SPA & SALON *Alchemy*

THE ULTIMATE GUIDE TO SPA & SALON OWNERSHIP

If

SPA & SALON *Alchemy*

THE ULTIMATE GUIDE TO SPA & SALON OWNERSHIP

By Sandra Alexcae Moren

THOMSON

DELMAR LEARNING

Australia   Canada   Mexico   Singapore   Spain   United Kingdom   United States

THOMSON

DELMAR LEARNING

Spa and Salon Alchemy

The Ultimate Guide to Spa & Salon Ownership

Sandra Alexcae Moren

MILADY STAFF

President:
Dawn Gerrain

Director of Editorial:
Sherry Gomoll

Developmental Editor:
Judy Aubrey Roberts

Editorial Assistant:
Jessica Burns

Director of Production
Wendy A. Troeger

Production Editor:
Eileen M. Clawson

Production Assistant:
Angela Iula

Composition:
Graphic World

Director of Marketing
Wendy E. Mapstone

Channel Manager:
Sandra Bruce

Marketing Coordinator:
Kasmira Koniszewski

Cover Design:
Suzanne Nelson, essence of 7 design

For permission to use material from this text or product, contact us by
Tel (800) 730-2214
Fax (800) 730-2215
www.thomsonrights.com

Any additional questions about permissions can be submitted by e-mail at thomsonrights@thomson.com.

Library of Congress Cataloging-in-Publication Data

Moren, Sandra Alexcae.
   Spa and salon alchemy : the ultimate guide to spa and salon ownership / by Sandra Alexcae Moren.
      p. cm.
   Includes bibliographical references and index.
   ISBN 1-4018-7955-1
   1. Beauty shops—Management. 2. Health resorts—Management. I. Title.

TT965.M69 2004
646.7'2'068—dc22   2004061015

NOTICE TO THE READER

Publisher does not warrant or guarantee any of the products described herein or perform any independent analysis in connection with any of the product information contained herein. Publisher does not assume, and expressly disclaims, any obligation to obtain and include information other than that provided to it by the manufacturer.

The reader is expressly warned to consider and adopt all safety precautions that might be indicated by the activities described herein and to avoid all potential hazards. By following the instructions contained herein, the reader willingly assumes all risks in connection with such instructions.

The publisher makes no representations or warranties of any kind, including but not limited to, the warranties of fitness for particular purpose or merchantability, nor are any such representations implied with respect to the material set forth herein, and the publisher takes no responsibility with respect to such material. The publisher shall not be liable for any special, consequential, or exemplary damages resulting, in whole or part, from the reader's use of, or reliance upon, this material.

This book is dedicated to:
My children, Dean, Tammy, and Dale; their spouses; and my wonderful grandchildren Kelsey, Elissa, Dylan, and Billie-Ann, who have brought me so much love and joy, taught me so much, always accepted me, and shared me with my career.

My brother, Dwayne, and his wife, Brenda, who have taught me so much about life and relationships.

All of you who play a part in this fabulous professional beauty service industry, which touches peoples' hearts and souls on a daily basis. You revitalize their body, mind, and spirit through the experiences you create for them.

About the Author

Sandra Alexcae Moren, B. Ed., owner of Kyron Spa and Salon Consulting, a division of Chiron Marketing Inc. <www.kyron.ca>, shares her 30-plus years of experience in the professional beauty industry. A member of the International Spa Association (ISPA) and a teacher and business owner for years, Sandra has taken her knowledge and in-depth, practical life experience and shared it in this book.

Her eclectic background also includes being a cosmetologist, educator, spa director, professional speaker, and master judge with the Judges Panel of Canada. She also has a Bachelor of Education Degree, with a major in Vocational Education and minors in Psychology and Drama, which she received from the University of Alberta. Sandra's diverse experience includes every aspect of spa and salon projects from inception to grand openings. You will find her at the drawing board with the design team, consulting with the accountant, standing on site with the contractors, sourcing equipment and products, creating treatments and services, writing Procedure Manuals, developing staff, and designing the marketing plan.

Throughout Sandra's life journey, her quest for truth and an avid interest in health and well-being led to a fascination with spirituality and alternative methods of healing. Working with indigenous cultures has truly been an honor and an incredible education, and her passion and love for her industry and humanity has blessed her with the ability to touch many individuals' spirits. Living, working, and traveling internationally have also allowed Sandra to personally experience and research in depth the diversity and dynamics of this evolving industry. As a result of these experiences Sandra believes spas and salons are healing centers, where individuals can experience a renewal of beauty, youthfulness, well-being, and rejuvenation . . . of body, mind, and spirit.

Creating this book to guide individuals to build their own spas and salons was a natural evolution for Sandra, who has an extensive background in writing articles for trade magazines, media promotional material, curriculum development, and corporate brochures. In this volume, she applies her elaborate professional knowledge, array of experiences, wisdom, and whimsical insight. Her passion, enthusiasm for life, and a belief in actualizing the human spirit has also enabled Sandra to inspire and transform others and make heart connections on her journey. The creation of this book took a lot of passion, commitment, persistence, discipline, creativity, and good old-fashioned hard work to become reality.

Acknowledgments

I want to sincerely thank the many individuals who have worked with me and supported me on this creative endeavor as well as those who contributed submissions to this project.

Special thanks to the fabulous team at Milady Publishing. Under the direction of Stephen Smith, acquisitions editor, the team worked very hard to make this dream a reality. Stephen, I appreciate your patience, understanding, and incredible support. Courtney VanAuskas, developmental editor, was always there for me, encouraging and patiently educating me on the various steps involved in publishing a book. Erica Conley, marketing assistant for career education SBU; Eileen Clawson, production editor; and Sandra Bruce, marketing channel manager, were always available, patient, and supportive.

My deepest appreciation to the professionals who took their valuable time to review this book:

Sheryl Baba, Solstice Day Spa, MA

Helen Bickmore, Jean Paul Spa, NY

Lenore Brooks, Brooks & Butterfield, Ltd., MA

Felicia Brown, Balance Day Spa, NC

Suzanne Mathis McQueen, The Phoenix, OR

Sandra Peoples, T.H. Pickens Tech, CO

Courtney Pippenger, Great Clips/Educator, TN

To Maureen Faber, a dear friend, a special lady, and my accountant who has kept me on track for more than 20 years, thank you for your friendship, spirituality, information, and faith in me.

To Cecilia Leatherberry, a dear friend and the architect of the Canadian Master Judges Program, thank you for the opportunity to be of service and for helping me learn so much from your program. From the beginning of my career and as it has evolved, you have been a mentor and a guiding light.

To Sherry Moir, a dear friend who entered my life in a very synchronistic way and became a powerful influence in my life, thank you for being there; helping in all the ways you do; and pushing me, which is natural for an Aries and a strong leader.

To Swan, a dear friend who allowed me to experience the aloha of Hawaii and swim with the dolphins, thank you for being such a kindred spirit and teaching me that pleasure and play are just as important as work.

To Hasoon Rahal, a dear friend and business client who let me express my creativity and expertise, thank you for allowing me the opportunity to help you develop the Spasation chain and for sharing your business acumen.

To Grace Lewis, a new friend who typed my handwritten pages, thank you for all your patience and hard work.

To Terry Willox, a dear friend and a brilliant man I call "The Wizard" who entered my life through Sherry Moir, thank you for taking the time and energy to understand me, accept me, and help me to focus my passion and creativity to get this book published and put my other dreams into action.

To Cynthia Bujold, a very special lady and dear friend who helped me pull this creative project together, thank you for all your hard work, formatting, reading, and so on. Most of all, thank you for your friendship, patience, faith, and support. You always seemed to know when I needed a friend.

To Moe Rahal, a very dear friend and extremely brilliant man, thank you for being you and taking time to read the manuscript. You challenged me and helped me to be more logical and thoughtful about situations and individuals.

To Gene Kosowan, who first edited the book, thanks for meeting deadlines and thanks for your patience. It has really evolved since the beginning.

To Darlene Mitansky, my Cappy friend and art director and owner of Wingspan Studio, who worked very hard to typeset this book, for your patience and understanding as we embarked on this journey together.

To Mary Ann Zapalic, a talented artist, for granting us permission to use her Chakra diagrams; and to Anodea Judith, author of *Wheels of Life*, for granting us permission to use her artwork.

Many thanks to Ernie Zelinski, an author who shared much information and ideas with me; Randy Morse, Kevin Burns, and others who edited the manuscript, including Dorothy Miller, Tracy Quinlan, Augustus Belcourt, Monica Wartenburg, Sheryl-Ann Lebsack, and Forrest Bard.

Thanks to all my friends, colleagues, clients, students, and business contacts who have been my greatest teachers and brought me a lot of joy.

Letter to the Reader

Keeping abreast of change and technology is a lifelong journey. Whether you are an educator, student, seasoned businessperson, health and wellness practitioner, stylist, aesthetician, manufacturer, or distributor—or if you are considering becoming a part of this dynamic spa and salon industry—the practical and insightful information in this definitive resource book will be beneficial.

Discover the emerging world views that will assist you in aligning your endeavor with the nouveauté trends. Basic challenges that the spa and salon industry as a whole are facing are identified. You will find solutions to various types of challenges you may be facing in these changing times.

This resource book can be used as a guide to help you design, build, develop, operate, and brand a highly profitable spa/salon business. Business systems are identified for reference, and appendices provide formats such as performance-based job descriptions, performance-based evaluations, contracts, company policy manual, and other tools for your personal use.

Both ancient and new innovative approaches to healing, longevity, well-being, beauty, and youthfulness are introduced to help you develop leading-edge spa/salon experiences for your clients. I am delighted to share the art of alchemy, which will give you an understanding of your personal role in the transformative aspects of body, mind, and spirit.

It is hoped that you will discover some ideas and information that you can use in fulfilling your personal dreams, whatever they may be. Enjoy, dare to dream, and find your passion!

Table of Contents

Preface

This book was created as a resource guide and educational tool to assist individuals within the Professional Beauty Industry and the Health and Wellness fields. It will be specifically valuable to the following:

- Educators and students studying hair, aesthetics, nails, massage, and spa and salon operations
- New and existing spa and salon owners, directors, management, and team members
- Manufacturers, suppliers, distributors, and salespeople who service the professional beauty industry and health and wellness fields

To keep abreast of the changes in this high-growth marketplace, it is vital to embrace lifelong learning and understand what is driving the phenomenal growth. This book is a result of more than 30-plus years of experience in the professional beauty industry. Throughout my years as a cosmetologist, educator, business owner, writer, professional speaker, and spa and salon consultant, I still remain the student, forever researching and learning. What keeps my passion for the industry is seeing the successes of my students and the clients I have assisted with their businesses and the relationships I have developed with my industry colleagues. Sharing my knowledge, research, and practical life experiences within this book evolved from extensive notes that I had kept over the years. This information is my personal perception based on all my years of diverse and direct involvement in the industry.

Topics featured in the book are as follows:

- Emerging world views, trends, and opportunities for the spa and salon industry

- Information on leasing, designing, developing, and operating a profitable business

- Business systems that are imperative to your business infrastructure

- How to lower your startup costs and boost your revenues to increase your profits

- How to market and brand your business in this highly competitive marketplace

- Processes involved to educate, coach, and develop the individual and how to attract and retain staff and clients

- Detailed leading-edge equipment lists and products that are available for your spa, salon, and aesthetic areas

- Ancient and new approaches to healing, longevity, well-being, beauty, and youthfulness

- An exploration of the spiritual anatomy or human energy systems and how they affect the physical body's structure

- An in-depth description of a wide variety of services and treatments that can be offered in the spa and salon

- Concepts for Consideration in every chapter, a glossary, and identification of trade magazines, associations, and Web sites

- Comprehensive appendices that include a sample Company Policy Manual, employee contract, application for employment, performance-based job descriptions, performance evaluations, recruitment system, candidate assessment record, contract agreement, and procedures manual outline

Having clarity of the trends and opportunities in the marketplace will give you the competitive edge. Whether you use the information offered is a matter of choice; the main intent is to provide you with timely knowledge so you are aware of what is out there and what is happening in our industry.

Nouveauté: Emerging World Views

The French have a word for it: **nouveauté,** which means newness, novelty, change and innovation—attributes that the spa/salon industry, and almost every other entrepreneurial venture in the economy for that matter, need to have to stay alive in these rapidly changing times. The "Information Age" and "New Economy" are not only changing the ways wealth is created; they are altering life as we know it. The Internet, for example, has become the global exchange for information and the vehicle for electronic commerce.

A **world view** is a way of arranging the infinite energy of the universe or information into a system that makes sense. Having an understanding of the emerging world views will help you stay abreast of consumer demands and new technology in the spa/salon industry.

Metamorphosis, the "magic of life," is the process of change that ensures growth and allows us to shed the old before we come into the new. The spa/salon culture is going through such a metamorphosis. If the industry embraces—rather than resists—these changes, we can expect a journey of transformation that evolves into insightful clarity. Being clear about these aspects of transformation will give you a better understanding of the strategies needed to align your business with what lies ahead.

A changing marketplace challenges individuals to understand and implement innovative processes to create business environments offering services, treatments, and products that are aligned with the New World views.

Knowledge Equals Excellence in Performance

In a future when many old rules will no longer apply, companies and industries with the most knowledgeable employees will excel in performance. Given the rapidly changing North American workforce and the fact that the amount of information being processed worldwide doubles every 18 months, lifelong learning will be an absolute necessity for players to keep abreast of changes and stay competitive. Businesses experiencing difficulties attracting and retaining highly skilled professional employees are slowly realizing the need to place more investment in human resources to adjust to an unpredictable economic environment.

Several corporations are responding by replacing past perks such as company cars and expense accounts with incentives such as laptops, high-quality training programs, tuition reimbursements, bonuses, profit-sharing schemes, stock purchase plans, and health benefit packages. Some even offer life assistance programs such as child care subsidies, backup day care, and mortgage support.

"The political, business and cultural bedrocks that anchored our lives are crumbling like stale scones," said **futurist** (an individual who studies different aspects of society and human development to discern the developing trends) and trend spotter Faith Popcorn in her book *Clicking*. Look around and you might find it hard to dispute her claim. Pillars of society, such as government, religion, education, health care, medicine, business, banking, marriage, and family, are all being questioned—sometimes even challenged—by individuals. When governments cannot balance budgets, churches are plagued by scandals and lawsuits, and large corporations are experiencing nightmares from accounting scandals to rampant downsizing, where does an individual turn for salvation?

Well, for starters, we might look toward something that has always been with us.

The Human Spirit and Alchemy

The importance of the human spirit was one discovery made by authors John Nasbitt and Patricia Aburdene in *Megatrends 2000*, published in 2000. In the book, the authors explored a New World perspective of a "respect for the human spirit" in which a revived spirituality could encourage members of society to seek answers to their problems by looking within themselves.

At a time when lives are spinning out of control—as a result of negative influences such as time famine, information overload, increasing market demands on personal productivity and performance, and lack of permanence and security—many people are starting to abandon their materialistic quests and search for solutions that may lie in spiritual traditions.

Wise physicians throughout history knew that body, mind, and spirit were connected.

> *"Soul and body, I suggest, react sympathetically upon each other. . .A change in the state of the soul produces a change in the state of the body, and conversely, a change in the state of the body produces a change in the state of the soul."*
>
> *Aristotle, 350 B.C.*

Now a new set of views is forming, creating a belief system that looks much like our ancient traditions, yet is reinforced and transformed by our modern sciences. For example, a recent medical theory, **energy medicine**—also dubbed **vibrational medicine**—is supported by the **Einsteinium world view,** which states that all matter is really another form of energy. In other words, human beings are viewed as unique energy systems rather than biologic machines.

> *"We have reached a point in our evolution that requires us to learn to speak energy fluently. Our search to understand the essence of health as well as our newfound passion to form a mature relationship with the spiritual dimensions of our lives has led us to this crossroad."*
>
> *Caroline Myss, PhD*

The mystique of the word alchemy has conjured up many ideas of its meaning. **Alchemy,** which connects health and longevity to metallurgy, dates back to ancient Egypt and Greece, although similar forms of the craft were evident in India and China. The alchemists realized the mystery was not outside, but in the psyche, the psychological and spiritual process of transformation. In the 1920s Carl Jung became fascinated with alchemy and theorized it was a "journey of the soul."

According to Jean Dubuis, founder and first president of the French Alchemical organization, The Philosophers of Nature:

> *"Alchemy is the Science of Life, of Consciousness. The alchemists know there is a very solid link between matter, life, and consciousness. Alchemy is the art of manipulating life and consciousness in matter to help it evolve or solve the problems of inner disharmony."*

Dubuis has an extensive professional career in electrical engineering for a major international firm in France; he has worked in the field of nuclear physics with Nobel Prize winner Irène Joliot-Curie and has actively practiced alchemy for more than 65 years.

On a material level, alchemists sought to find a physical process to convert base metals such as lead to gold. Early alchemists were the forerunners of our modern sciences, chemistry and physics. On a spiritual level, alchemists worked to purify themselves by eliminating the *base* material of self and achieving the *gold* of enlightenment. Therefore, we can define alchemy as an ancient path of transformation and spiritual purification, which expands the **consciousness** (awareness, cognizance, and knowingness) and develops insight and intuition. Thanks to research into the structure of matter and the behavior of energy, scientists now understand that the basic underlying reality behind all existence is not matter, but consciousness—a common thread in ancient mystical teachings.

Individuals are recognizing the importance of health and wellness as life spans increase. Because our culture is gravitating toward greater inner exploration and integration of body, mind, and spirit, people are open to new approaches to healing, longevity, and youthfulness. With increasing interest in holistic and preventive health care, the appeal of the spa/salon industry has grown. The majority of individuals want to look good, feel good, and retain their youth and vitality as long as possible.

Electromagnetic Medicine Reemerging as a Viable Therapy

The emerging world view is that matter is energy operating at different frequencies. Dr. Robert O. Becker, twice nominated for the Nobel Prize and best known for his 1985 book *The Body Electric,* demonstrated that optimal amounts of electromagnetic energy flowing through the body would determine the level of your health. This discovery, he points out, is the basis for **electromagnetic medicine,** a new treatment that could represent the future of health care—a bridge between Eastern and Western cultures, ancient and modern civilizations, spirit and matter. Becker's findings are based on earlier discoveries by electronic pioneer Nicola Tesla, who in 1889 discovered the therapeutic amenities of electrical frequencies on living organisms.

Tina Emily Phillips, in her article, "Electro Regeneration Therapy" <www.biotronix.net>, wrote the following:

"Although vibrational energy medicine is commonly thought of as acupuncture, homeopathy, etc., it also includes therapeutic methods that apply frequency information directly to the body with electricity, sound, color, and lights. This is the rapidly evolving field of Electro-Medicine. For much of the twentieth century, the chemical-mechanistic model of the biological system has ruled both the medical and the scientific establishments. Now, as a result of ground-breaking research into the mysteries of cellular growth, healing, and regeneration, a new paradigm is emerging."

Dr. Bruce Hoffman, of the Hoffman Centre of Integrative Medicine in Calgary, Alberta, Canada, believes the following:

"Alternative medicine is being integrated into mainstream medicine by patient-driven, educated consumerism, whether the medical profession likes it or not. Patients are no longer tolerant of alternative medicine being regarded as light medicine. They are taking their holistic world views seriously and expecting their health care providers to assist them. People are realizing they are more than a physical body with a set of symptoms. They have an electromagnetic body that is environmentally influenced; a more subtle body comprised of the mind, intellect, and ego; a soul that is immortal and beyond space and time."

Now, contrast this exciting discovery with a more sobering trend.

How Sick Is the Health Care Industry?

According to Canada's Federal Health Minister, health care costs are rapidly compromising the ability of provinces in the country to provide other necessary services, such as education and welfare and basic infrastructure such as road building. With costs skyrocketing from $42.4 billion in 1990 to $68 billion in 2001, the current health care system has focused more on acute treatment rather than preventive care.

In the United States, where the industry generates more than $1 trillion in business annually, expenditures are expected to almost triple by 2010. In 2000 the American Association of Health Plans indicated that roughly 700,000 seniors would be axed from their Medicare Choice HMOs. Although health care for seniors is not seen as a profitable venture, the association said the problem will only get worse when 75 million baby boomers reach their golden years within the next decade.

According to Kailee Kline, Founding President of the Association of Premier Spas of Ontario and owner of HealthWinds, the Health and Wellness Spa in Toronto, Ontario:

"In the last three years, we have witnessed the emergence of the Wellness industry in Canada, driven by an enormous market demand for quality assured health and wellness services and products. National studies have confirmed that the demand for Spa services has exceeded those for skiing and golf. In Canada, extended health benefits and the professionalism of our complementary health disciplines, and evolving healthcare priorities of an aging population have helped to make the Spa accessible and credible to many on a regular basis. It is quickly becoming a 'sought after and must have lifestyle choice.'"

Kailee has worked in the industry for more than 25 years and has seen countless changes.

Fortunately, many healing centers around the world are offering alternatives. While living on the magnificent Big Island of Hawaii, I toured an incredible, state-of-the-art healing facility in Waimea. The North Hawaii Community Hospital is a full-service, acute-care, community-owned, nonprofit hospital that opened in May 1996 to serve the 30,000 residents and visitors of the island's northern region. Designed as a healing instrument, the hospital is fast becoming a prototype for the careful integration of select complementary healing practices with high-quality medical care.

"Our vision at North Hawaii Community Hospital is to treat the whole individual—body, mind, and spirit—with a team approach to patient-centered care and ultimately become the most healing hospital in the world," said Jonathan Guilbert, the hospital's team leader in marketing-development. "We offer a full spectrum of acute care hospital services that take into consideration family, culture, and community. We value our environment of aloha, which nurtures trust, respect, self-expression, open minds, and hearts."

Patients warm up to the facility's healing environment, which features natural lighting and garden views via lanai doors in every patient room. Common areas are illuminated by skylights and windows, and landscaped gardens, courtyards, and other areas incorporate warm colors, textures, and art into their interior design to reflect a homelike ambiance. There is even an incredible meditation room that radiates a serene energy.

At the hospital, patients have access to a full range of amenities, including art; music; audiovisual materials on healing, humor, and relaxation and visualization techniques; spiritual counseling; and healing touch (a noninvasive therapy of specialized touching techniques that assess and treat the energy systems of the patient, who is fully clothed during the procedure). Licensed complementary healers are also on staff, specializing in naturopathy, acupuncture, massage therapy, clinical psychology, and chiropractic medicine.

We have so much to learn about facility design and healing sanctuaries, such as what is offered at North Hawaii Community Hospital.

Using Trends as Tools

The good news is that if we can sift through all the information and use the relevant knowledge, we can discern trends. The futurists are always studying different aspects of society and human development to see what trends are developing. "It is trends that drive your business and your life," says Faith Popcorn.

As these trends emerge, consumers will drive the marketplace. Using demographics, which are the statistical characteristics of a human population, is the most powerful tool we have to understand the past and to predict the future. The more knowledge you have about demographic realities, the better prepared you are to find ways to capitalize on them.

What is the marketplace for the spa/salon industry? The baby boomers are still the most dominant group—almost 10 million out of 30 million Canadians. Their offspring, the echo kids, total 6.5 million and are the second most important group. Because the entire North American marketplace is dominated by boomers and their children, the facts suggest that the most rapidly growing markets in the following decades will be for services and products used by them. Middle-aged boomers perceive themselves as more youthful than previous generations were at the same age. Cosmetic surgery is being used by most generations, especially by boomers who are rapidly losing the youthful appearance many of them value so highly.

A mature population is more demanding and more knowledgeable about services and products they need and desire and will not tolerate poor service or lack of professionalism. The boomers have grown up in a retail environment where quality services and products are demanded and delivered faster than ever before. They expect to have their photos processed in an hour, not in a day, and they expect high-quality results or they will not accept them. In the meantime, lack of knowledge and education in the spa/salon industry by owners, directors, managers, and employees is eroding trust, credibility, and integrity in consumers' minds.

If professionals in the spa/salon industry are to succeed today, they need to understand two basic phenomena:

- Customers are very knowledgeable, are well-traveled, and demand quality services and products for their dollar.
- Services and products of excellent quality need to be matched with well-educated and trained employees who are able to inform and explain everything a customer desires to know.

Lynne Walker McNees, executive director of the International Spa Association (ISPA), says the following:

"Consumer demand is driving the spa explosion. Consumers are much more savvy now about the spa experience and they are busier than ever before; they are looking for a one-stop-shop. When someone goes to a health or fitness centre, a resort or hotel, or a salon, they want a place where they can get it all, which often includes having a spa treatment. Medical spas are definitely an emerging trend. Now a woman or man can get their annual physical, and at the same time, treat themselves to a relaxing massage or facial. ISPA defines the spa experience as your time to relax, reflect, revitalize, and rejoice, with the key words being your time. Consumers simply have to take the time for themselves in order to be better people for their families, friends, and coworkers."

With the emerging world views and the many mysteries of the universe being understood, the consequence of being aligned with your own **frequency,** which dictates the creation and quality of cell tissue, may allow you to mature and not age as quickly. By becoming congruent with spirit, you may alter your relationship with time and space. The consequence of new realities may be compared to proving the world is round when everyone thought it was flat.

This is a very confusing marketplace for many businesses and consumers. You need to mentally distance yourself, step back, question, research, and analyze it. The aspects of nouveauté—possibility thinking, creativity, and innovation—become very important when positioning yourself and your business in relation to the transformations taking place in our society. Ultimately, it depends on you to educate yourself on the changes and decide whether you agree or disagree with these changes. *But like it or not, the transformations are already happening.*

The question remains: how do we make sense of these transformations and capitalize on the trends? The industry is left with two daunting choices: *ignore the emerging world views and be left behind, or capitalize on those trends as effectively as you can and stay competitive.*

That is exactly what the information and essence of this book addresses.

Concepts for Consideration

1. Consider ways that the Einsteinium world view might be expressed in your spa/salon concept.
2. How would offering alternative services benefit your spa/salon?
3. How would you make use of the demographic realities in developing your spa/salon business?
4. What is the benefit to the spa/salon professional in understanding the behaviors and demands of today's consumers?
5. How does continuous learning and education for your staff benefit your spa/salon?

Develop a Profitable Business

To develop a business for profitability you need to identify all the components of a business. The first stage is building the facility; the second stage is building the infrastructure of your business with systems; and the final stage is implementing the systems you have created consistently. According to Michael E. Gerber, author of *The E-Myth,* "The key is to plan, envision, and articulate what you see in the future both for yourself and your employees. Because if you don't articulate it—I mean, write it down clearly, so others can understand it—you don't own it! And do you know that in all the years I've been doing this work with small business owners, out of the thousands upon thousands we've met, there have been few who had any plans at all!"

The emergence of a new economy brings **transformation** (a change in structure, appearance, or character) to the world of business. Seasoned business professionals never presume to know the truth; they are always questioning whether what was true yesterday is applicable today or to the future. To pursue the boundless opportunities around, you must open your mind to the wide range of possibilities out there.

The Process of Change

We face change in every aspect of our lives. We see companies and organizations collapse because of their inability to change their ways of thinking and behaving. Individuals experience frustration when they have not spent time anticipating changes and responding to the need for adjustment.

As the world changes around us, we need to rethink our **perceptions** and move to new levels of discernment regarding business; people; and body, mind, and spirit. Our perceptions, the mindset we use to view the world, and how we view ourselves are shaped by our personal experiences, education, and beliefs. **Discernment**—a process involving perception, intuition, decision making, and action—is the ability to differentiate between making choices and making decisions. Rethinking our beliefs, purposes, priorities, and patterns of behaving moves us to new levels of discernment. For example, if you are always in a crisis, driven by projects under deadline and putting out fires, what behaviors could you change to produce different results?

Any transformation, like learning, results in a change of awareness, **consciousness** (awareness, cognizance, and knowingness), action, and behavior. For transformation to take place, we need to examine three levels of mastery:

1. Being open to new ideas, information, and consciousness
2. Integrating this new information into our lives
3. Taking actions and using discipline, integrity, and focus to create results of your choosing

The spa/salon industry is in an ideal position to put these levels of mastery to work. In 2001, the International Spa Association (ISPA) reported that the U.S. industry raked in $10.7 billion in revenue, eclipsing box office receipts and amusement and theme park admissions that same year. That is more than double the revenue figures of $5 billion reported in 1999 for the spa/salon industry.

"The spa industry has solidified itself as a major player in the hospitality and leisure sector," reported the ISPA in its *2002 Spa Industry Study.* "Despite the economic downturn, the industry has continued to grow at a robust pace."

The news gets even better for the 10,000 spas in North America, roughly three-fourths of them operating as day spas. "Many people are no longer seeing spas as 'pampering,' but as a necessity in order to stay healthy," stated the report, alluding to the opportunities for the industry to introduce its services to the health care sector.

Even more encouraging was this assessment in the report: "Spas are now seen as trendy to own by wealthy individuals, just as restaurants were in the '80s and bars/clubs in the '90s." the report. According to the Price Waterhouse Coopers 2000 Spa Industry Growth Study, "Virtually every facet of the spa industry is growing at an incredible pace." It also recognized the expansion of the industry and identified specific basic areas that could improve its development:

1. Clarify industry language and communication—consumers are confused about "what a spa really is" and the types and benefits of treatments available.

2. Emphasize good health rather than indulgences.

3. Pay attention to appearance improvement because of the "youth mentality" of corporate America.

4. Pay attention to "spiritual needs" of consumers.

5. "Dedicate to a higher purpose" beyond business and marketing.

6. Form partnerships with medical communities and alternative healers.

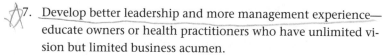

7. Develop better leadership and more management experience— educate owners or health practitioners who have unlimited vision but limited business acumen.

8. Solve the problem of scarcity of qualified personnel and trouble recruiting and retaining qualified employees.

9. Develop creative compensation strategies and professional education/training to build employee loyalty.

10. Educate employees averse to sales and solve the problem of inability to generate retail sales and not capitalizing on necessary home-maintenance products.

11. Generate sufficient cash flow and develop marketing expertise to manage complexity and expense of operating spas.

12. Be able to provide a unique experience while managing labor and operating costs such as "cost per spa treatment."

13. Manage the fact that spa margins of profitability are relatively small and debt service is large.

14. Make sourcing products, equipment, and consultants less confusing.

The most perilous period in an industry's development is when it shows the following:

1. Wild growth

2. High earnings

3. Rapid sales growth

These three elements breed mistakes masked by outside prosperity. When we can identify specific areas that need to change in the business, effective strategies can be implemented.

It then becomes your responsibility as an owner, manager, director, or employee to make the necessary choices and changes.

Create and Develop Your Business

What is your perception of business? How would you define it? A business is an organization that strives to provide an adequate profit return for the owner or investor while meeting the needs of its employees and customers. Visionary entrepreneurs are leaders who create and build an organization; *it is that organization that builds the business.*

Every business goes through three stages of development: infancy, adolescence, and adulthood. A business at the infancy stage needs to be fed, watched, guarded, and nurtured constantly. It is still vulnerable and has to be tended to without providing much in return. If you are patient and can stick to a plan, your baby becomes an adolescent. At this stage, it starts to support itself. Finally, with patience, perseverance, and a strong vision, you will reach your goals and the adult stage. It will mature powerfully, with the ability to support you and others abundantly. Remember that growth should be slow and steady—do not draw out too much or expand too quickly. You become the "Master Builder" using common sense and acquired knowledge combined with practical planning and systematically proceeding step-by-step to reach your goals.

"The sower may mistake and sow his seeds crookedly; the peas make no mistake, but come up and show his line."

Ralph Waldo Emerson

"A good product or brilliant founder alone does not make a company," says Michael Cooper, president of the Hay Group's Research for Management. "Success comes when leaders have managed their people in ways that keep their involvement and sense of partnership high. Keeping people 'excited' is the leader's job."

"Leaders who believe they must continuously scurry about motivating everyone are destined to a fatiguing ulcerating career," adds Robert Wright, a professor of Organization Theory at California's Pepperdine University. Ultimately, you want employees who are self-directed, who are eager to accomplish their tasks, who cannot wait to get something done, and who are always enthusiastic.

The most exciting breakthroughs of the twenty-first century will occur not because of technology but because of an exploding concept of what it means to be human and how to actualize human potential. Leaders will build followership through having professional integrity, being authentic, valuing the human spirit, possessing strong business acumen, and creating an environment where the unique potentials of the employees will be expressed.

Tradeskill: The Entrepreneur's Sixth Sense

Michael Phillips and Salli Raspberry explored a novel look at how human potential could be applied to business in their book, *Honest Business*. While putting together the content, the duo coined the term **"tradeskill"** to refer to an experimental, hands-on, common sense, sixth-sense approach to business.

Tradeskill is what you learn as a kid working in open-air markets. It is how the horse traders of old closed deals and how merchants developed their moxie for hustling. Tradeskill gives you insight into understanding what people want; how much they will pay; how to read marketplace signals; and how to approach a given product, market, or niche. Those who have a sixth sense for business are able to make decisions quickly, cutting through months of meetings, brainstorming, market studies, and bureaucratic shuffling. They also know how to handle money—how to buy and how to pay.

Tradeskill cannot be learned in a masters of business administration program. It comes from hands-on experience and is part of our innate being. At the heart of tradeskill is the ability to see events around you in a detached, pragmatic way. If you are starting or running a business by pinning your hopes on some theory that the world will beat a path to your door, you are in trouble. If you do not think you have tradeskill in your blood, consider going into business with someone who does. Tradeskill people are lateral thinking multitaskers who intuitively know the steps and connect the dots in an abstract yet sequential, step-by-step process.

An example of tradeskill in action is the success story of Hasoon Rahal. Immigrating to Canada from his native Lebanon when he was only 14, Hasoon worked for 20 years in the hair industry until he came across the notion that the Edmonton market was sophisticated enough for a European spa model. He also felt that if he offered the same first-class service to all customers regardless of status or wealth, his business would flourish.

He was right on both counts. Today, his chain of four Edmonton-based Spasation spa/salons—operating under the motto "affordable and indulgent for everyone"—gross $4.5 million annually and receive as many as 1,200 clients daily.

To accommodate his growing clientele, Hasoon has finished a $300,000 renovation to one Spasation branch in Edmonton's Londonderry district to include 17 treatment rooms and a large retail area on its 12,000-square-foot premises. He is also embarking on an $8.5 million expansion program, including establishing spas in other Canadian cities such as Calgary, Vancouver, Winnipeg, and Montreal, where, at this writing, he is negotiating leases. He also plans to add Turkish baths to three of the new locations.

"This is the real treatment, like Phoenicians and ancient kings used to experience," claims Hasoon about the reason for Spasation's success. "The key to good service is pampering clients with personal attention in a subdued ambiance with porcelain-tiled floors, muted lighting, soft classical music, plenty of flowers, antiques, and loving care. You get treated like a queen or king, whether you are rich or poor." Hasoon predicted that Spasation, currently with a staff of 275, including 10 at a call center, will have 800 employees once the last of the nine new locations are rolled out by the end of 2005.

Visionary entrepreneurs know one thing: change is the norm and only the adaptable will survive. Business will become an arena where you consciously interact and build relationships with others for the mutual growth of all concerned.

Maybe you already have a spa/salon and want to improve specific areas of concern, or perhaps you are building or purchasing a business. Whatever the scenario, some basic business fundamentals and management systems can be helpful for your success and profitability.

Business Systems

One very important fundamental principle, if integrated into your personal and business life on a daily basis, will bring amazing results. It is called the *Pareto Principle*, more commonly known as the *20/80 Rule:*

Priorities: 20 percent of your priorities give you 80 percent of your production.

Time: 20 percent of your time produces 80 percent of the results.

Products: 20 percent of the products bring in 80 percent of the profit.

Activities: 20 percent of your activities give you 80 percent of your results.

Leadership: 20 percent of the people will exemplify 80 percent of the leadership qualities.

The question is where, what, why, when, and how will you invest time, energy, and money as a businessperson? Systematic approaches are 80 percent of quality customer service and allow you to consistently give customers what they want. Creating, designing, applying, implementing, and monitoring such systems are the most important way to provide professional quality service.

Let us look at and analyze the system you have in place right now in your business and the ones you might decide are important enough to establish. Categorizing and defining a systematic method of business infrastructure will be personalized to your individual beliefs, knowledge, and organizational needs.

Individual systems become a part of the whole organization and overlap, working together to create synergy (see box on page 18). The processes used to identify the specific systems are varied for better clarification and understanding. You may choose to categorize the system elements differently. In the appendices, sample formats are provided that can be customized for your organization.

Financial System

Almost every business person has experienced being told by a banker, investor, or consultant to do a business plan when they have shared a business idea or dream. Most individuals get an overwhelming feeling of discomfort when they are given all the papers to read over and forms to complete. Frustration sets in once you actually begin reading the information and completing the first part: name and type of business.

Those feelings are natural responses because the ability to write a business plan may not be your forte. You should invest in an accountant who can also act as your financial and tax consultant. The accountant's expertise is required for monitoring the business plan, taxes, financial statements analysis, and the progress of your business. Your accountant relies on the information you provide when he or she creates the financial projections.

Financial System

- Foundation of business fundamentals necessary to effectively run a profitable and successful business
- Business plan
- Financial statements
- Budgets

Operating System

- Identify suppliers, equipment, and product needs
- Ordering procedures, inventory control
- Product/service profile
- Payroll system
- Gift certificates

Personnel System

- Procedures and methods that can be implemented to improve recruitment, training, and retaining staff
- Company policy manual
- Employee contract
- Procedures manual
- Application form
- Job descriptions
- Employee performance evaluation
- Recruitment system
- Interview system
- Training/education programs

Marketing, Research, and Development

- Marketing program
- Budget and yearly planning
- Strategies for researching and developing
- Renewing and evolving business strategies, marketing strategies, products, services/treatments, and equipment

It has been my experience that some individuals building a spa do not give all the relevant information necessary to have a viable business plan. Some examples include not accurately costing out your equipment and not deciding on or costing out treatments and services. How can you project income without knowing your profit on services and treatments?

Your business plan is a picture of your idea or dream that clarifies the business, the direction you are going, how you will get there, and the projected results. It provides a blueprint for future growth and is a key document necessary for investors. It also gives you, the owner, the realistic viability of the business.

Business plans are always evolving. Remember, it is always easier to see profit on paper. Regardless of the size of your business, generating enough profit to continue to evolve should be your goal. Financial intelligence is seeing the big picture. It is *not* about how much money you make; it is about *how much money you keep*. It is about return on investment and responsibility to your employees and customers who believe in your leadership and business acumen. Clients of mine have phoned me, exclaiming excitedly, "I made $300,000 this month!" I respond, "Great, tell me how much you actually have left after expenses." Or, "What percentage of profit are you up from the preceding month?"

Everything is relative. I know small businesses that generate more profit than large, fancy corporations.

"Unhappiness comes from not facing some reality that you need to face squarely."

Buddhist saying

People do not go into business to fail. What they often do is to go into business without full understanding of all the skills required and their odds of surviving. New small business owners should bear in mind that 50 percent fail during the first year and 90 percent fail in less than 5 years. In Canada, statistical analyses of small business failures show that the following causes make up more than 95 percent of the failures:

1. Lack of competence to manage the business
2. Lack of experience in that type of business and unbalanced experience
3. Lack of managerial experience

In addition, the following specific problems are identified:

1. Inability to find competent employees
2. Poor location
3. Pressure from large competitors
4. Failure to organize and plan
5. Inadequate starting capital
6. Inadequate working capital

7. High operating expenses

8. Tax burdens

9. Limited credit from suppliers

10. Inability to finance expansion

11. Expanding too fast or setting up other locations without a secure base operation

12. Inability to keep proper accounting records

More than 50 percent of the items mentioned are directly related to financial factors. Most aspects are eventually reflected in one way or another in the financial statements—and the inability to interpret, analyze, and make decisions about information presented by the financial statements and related financial information. The benefits and value in creating, understanding, and implementing a financial system will reflect in the business profit. Business plans have variations, yet there are common expectations.

Let us look at relevant and basic financial systems. A bonus for the spa/salon industry is that you have no accounts receivable. How would you feel if you had to wait 30, 60, or 90 days to be paid for services rendered? We need to count our blessings for the cash basis of the industry. Distributors and other accounts receivable businesses are not so lucky; they often have to wait for you to pay them. Meanwhile, they have expenses such as rent, salaries, and so on to handle.

You will need a day-to-day system for depositing your revenue and a method for paying expenses. Whether you personally handle your finances or let your bookkeeper do the job, you will need to rely on some type of monthly budget. We all know about budgets and how sometimes they are difficult to live within because of unforeseen circumstances. A budget will take those situations into account and provide you with a guideline for how much you can spend each month against your earnings the previous month as well as the earnings needed this month to meet next month's expenses. If you are using a computer in your business, you can find great software management packages that, if used effectively, will help you assess all the required information. *Understanding your financial information and controlling your dollars is the key to making money in your business.*

Financial Statements

The two major components of a set of financial statements are the **balance sheet** (a financial document that gives you the financial position of

BUSINESS PLAN

1. Company description
   - Name
   - Structure . . .: Proprietorship, Corporation, Limited Partnership
   - Vision/Mission/Philosophy Statement
2. Expertise specialists
   - Banker
   - Consultant
   - Lawyer
   - Accountant
3. Product and service description
4. Financial system
   - Startup costs and financial requirements
   - 1–3-year financial projection, including financial statement (balance sheet and income statement) and cash flow
   - Sales and net income projections
   - Assumptions to identify the financial forecast
5. Personnel system
   - Personnel to be hired and their salaries, commissions, and benefits
   - Training/education
6. Operating system
   - Suppliers, distributors, manufacturers, and other relevant businesses you will work with
   - Payroll system
   - Gift certificate system
   - Product, service, and treatment pricing
7. Marketing system
   - Plan
   - Analyze
   - Budget
8. Executive summary
   - Condensed version of the business plan including your mission statement
   - Written last but appears first in the business plan

the business, the assets, where the money came from, and what you did with the money) and the **income statement** (a financial statement that shows revenue, expenses, and profit during a given accounting period, usually either quarterly or yearly). Your accountant prepares the statements, but you, as a businessperson, need to learn to analyze and understand the information they offer you about your business.

Financial Statement

Income Statement
- Revenue − Expenses = Profit/Loss
- Can look good, while the cash flow puts you under
- Accounts receivable and purchasing assets

Balance Sheet
- Financial condition of a firm at any given date
- Lists assets, liabilities, and equities (value of firm)

In this industry, the only accounts receivable may be in the form of massage insurance claims. If you have an effective system for recording and processing the claims, you will have a fast turnaround. The insurance should be in place before the staff is paid.

Gift certificates can be confusing for some individuals. They are *not* classified as revenue at the time of purchase; they become revenue when they are redeemed. The money should be placed in a trust account until they are redeemed. It is similar to purchasing a house from a realtor. The lawyer puts the deposit in a trust account. If you sold $50,000 of gift certificates and your clients had 6 months to 1 year to use that gift certificate, you may believe you can use that surplus cash. What happens when the certificates are redeemed over the time period and you need to pay staff and product costs? How does that affect your budget? Understanding basic financial statements provides financial confidence and maturity about revenue so you can make corrections when things are not going as expected financially.

Analyzing the Income Statement

The income statement is a financial statement that shows revenue, expenses, and profit during a given accounting period, usually either quarterly or yearly. See the following expense analysis as an example (see box).

To make a profit you must know the variable costs for providing the service and apply a *percentage* of the fixed cost to every sale and *add on a percentage for profit*. Income statements expressed in dollars can provide useful information to the owner for monitoring the progress of the business operations and to make changes, particularly if done on a monthly basis.

Sometimes it is useful to convert the dollar information on income statements to "common size," meaning dollars are converted to a percentage basis.

$$\frac{\text{Net Profit}}{\text{Sales}} \times 100 = \% \text{ Net Profit by percentage of sales}$$

Then compare income statements for the preceding month, quarter, or year to get a true picture of the net profit.

Income statements show you the true profit—as opposed to cash profit—you might have calculated by looking at the amount of dollars left at the end of the month.

Analyzing the Balance Sheet

The balance sheet gives you a picture of the financial position of the business. Most business people look at the income statement; accountants and financial analysts look first at the balance sheet. It gives details on where you got the money represented by the assets on the balance sheet and what you did with it. The balance sheet also tells if you are living on borrowed money (and perhaps, borrowed time) and not the earnings of the business.

Fixed Costs
- Rent
- Utilities
- Phone
- Insurance
- Taxes
- Accounting, legal
- Financing costs
- Banking, machine fees (fixed machine fees [Visa, debit, etc.])
- Salaries, benefits
- Basic wage for commissioned staff

Variable Costs
- Products
- Commissioned staff
- Advertising

Cash flow is an accounting term defining all the cash received from all sources (within a specified period) and deducts from the cash what you have to pay out in that same period. When you do this, you will see the following:

1. Whether you have enough cash to make payments
2. How much cash you have on hand to begin activities next month

This is where large amounts of gift certificate money can be deceiving, if recorded as income or revenue.

At the beginning, and throughout its life, every business must produce accurate financial statements at least every 3 months. You simply cannot get away with the annual statements that go with your tax returns. Within a year, simple errors in the pricing of products and services can bankrupt the business.

Operating System

We are very lucky to have some excellent suppliers, distributors, and manufacturers in the industry. You need to create working relationships with the companies that are committed and supportive of your business. Can they ship you equipment such as hydraulic chairs within a week of being ordered and in the quantity and colors requested? Can they create custom products using the finest materials? Can they design a custom spa/salon environment that is ideal for your clientele? Can they offer an extensive range of products and services at competitive prices? If prospective suppliers and distributors can answer "yes" to all these questions, you have the makings of a healthy relationship.

When it comes to big-ticket items like spa/salon equipment, computers, management systems, washers, and dryers, find out the guarantee and maintenance processes and procedures. Sometimes getting the best deal up front does not turn out to be such a good bargain in the long run if these guarantees are not backed up by expertise, knowledge, and service.

For example, a Swiss shower became a very costly and frustrating experience for a spa owner. After the first day of operation, the owner realized there was not enough hot water in the facility to operate it while providing all the other available services. To make matters worse, the facility's design could not accommodate the installation of larger hot water tanks to keep the shower running. This forced the owner to completely tear out the shower, which ironically was relatively cheap to install compared to the costs of construction and removal. That particular sale soured the owner's willingness to deal with that particular company, who initially advised him that everything would be fine with his water supply. As an owner you need to build a relationship with clear communication and negotiate the guarantees, payment terms, credit limits, finance charges, and discounts with suppliers and distributors.

Some suppliers can help you with co-operative advertising, which is provided by certain manufacturers. Co-op advertising can be shared costs of advertising or a percentage of credit. You can find a few suppliers, who through the manufacturers can provide displays, bags, posters, and free samples.

Depending on the size and structure of the business, your ordering procedures and inventory control will be individualized. In small, owner-operated businesses, usually the owner will do the ordering. In larger chains with several locations, one person usually handles the ordering. With a spa/salon management software system, you input the inventory and amounts and then run the reports every week to find out what products you need. Retail inventory is always easier to control than back/bar products (those used at the sink area), chemicals in the salon, and the supplies in the professional cabinet (products used for the professional treatments).

Product and Service Profile

If you cannot design a system, hire someone to design it; you will save thousands of dollars in waste and theft. Prepacked spa treatments work well, but you are paying for the packaging. Mud bought in large quantities can be premeasured, prepacked, placed in containers, and placed in zip-close bags. This system was used effectively in a large spa in Scottsdale, Arizona, that has a massage staff of 70. Operating costs in the spa area have to be monitored closely because the equipment and overhead costs are higher than in the salon area.

Pricing of products and services are misunderstood in our industry. Retail products are usually marked up from 50 percent to 100 percent, depending on a number of variables, including overhead and location. Most people believe if they mark up a product 100 percent, they are making a profit of 100 percent. In reality, when you add your costs, you may be making a profit of only 10 percent.

To make a **profit** (revenue that is left over after subtracting the variable costs and a percentage of the fixed costs), you must do as follows:

- Know the **variable costs** (expenses that vary over the month) for providing the service.
- Apply a percentage of the **fixed cost** (expenses that remain the same every month) to every sale.
- Add on a percentage for profit.

Fixed and variable costs equal the operating costs, which are subtracted from the sale. An accountant can help you determine your operating costs into a relevant percentage and the markup you require to run your business profitably.

Spa services are not effectively cost calculated because of elements such as size of the treatment room, high equipment costs, and required supplies and products. Every square foot being paid for in rent needs to generate a certain amount of dollars. Your formula for figuring out costs per square foot versus sales per square foot is relevant to the individual business.

Formulas for pricing retail products are easy to figure out. Depending on your method, however, they can be deceiving (see box).

Salon service pricing is unique to the individual salon and what the market will bear. A haircut can range from $10 to $125.

When you perform a spa service, the variables included in operating expenses can be costly. A spa service uses robes, slippers, towels, linens (which need to be laundered), candles, fresh flowers, food/snacks, and oils in diffusers, plus the product cost. All of these must be determined to calculate the percentage of operating costs (see box for an example).

Using the same figures and different formulas is very deceiving when you do not consider operating costs. Some spas calculate their profit like Option B, when employees are commissioned 50 percent. In Option B the owner had not taken into consideration the employee deductions.

With the same treatment but different calculations there is a 30 percent difference in profit. In reality, the profit is 15 percent (if that), not the 50 percent commission. Why are we losing money on spa treatments and services? Perform your personal calculations for your hydrotherapy tub treatments, and have your accountant help you. Consider the fixed cost (of the tub) and operating costs.

Doing your business plan and actually taking the time to properly calculate your costs are vitally important. *Design a system based on product control. Imagine if the employee used 3 cups of mud rather than the allotted amount.*

Gift Certificates

Gift certificates are such wonderful creations, and we know by their popularity how many individuals enjoy them. The certificate itself can be a work of art, with textured paper, embossing, or fabric, depending on your budget. Regardless of what your certificates look like, quality control in your operating system for handling them is extremely important. You need to create a good numbering system to monitor the distribution of gift certificates. It is easy to have a dishonest employee exchange gift certificates for products under processes of cross marketing—which involves setting

RETAIL PRICE FORMULA

$$\text{Profit} = \frac{(\text{Selling Price} - \text{Cost})}{\text{Selling Price}} \times 100$$

Option A (Includes Cost & Expenses)

Shampoo Cost	$10.00
Operating Expense	$3.00
Total Cost & Expense	$13.00
Mark Up (70%)	+$9.10
Selling Price	$22.10

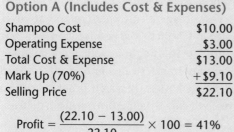

$$\text{Profit} = \frac{(22.10 - 13.00)}{22.10} \times 100 = 41\%$$

Option B (Includes Cost Only)

Shampoo Cost	$10.00
Mark Up (70%)	+$7.00
Selling Price	$17.00

$$\text{Profit} = \frac{(17.00 - 10.00)}{17.00} \times 100 = 41\%$$

■ Mark up on both options is 70%, both attain a profit margin of 41% but only option A is a true account since it incorporates actual cost plus expenses. When we incorporate actual cost and expenses to option B, the profit decreases as per example below.

■ **Option B (Includes Cost & Expense)**

Shampoo Cost	$10.00
(Actual Cost + Expense)	
Mark Up (70%)	+$7.00
Selling Price	$17.00

$$\text{Profit} = \frac{(17.00 - 13.00)}{17.00} \times 100 = 24\%$$

MUD TREATMENT FORMULA

Option A

Price of mud treatment		$60.00
1½ cups mud (cost)	$4.00	
Labor (cost)	$30.00	
Cost of treatment	$34.00	
Operating costs (50%)	$17.00	
Cost of mud treatment		$51.00
Profit		$9.00

$$\text{Profit \%} = \frac{\$9.00}{\$60.00} \times 100 = 15\% \text{ Profit}$$

Option B (Mistaken Profit)

Price of mud treatment	$60.00
Less 1½ cups mud (cost)	− $4.00
Sub Total	$56.00
Less Labor Commission (50%)	−$28.00
Profit	$28.00

$$\text{Profit \%} = \frac{\$28.00}{\$60.00} \times 100 = 47\%$$

up alliances with other businesses so you can mutually benefit. Any fraudulent practices will show up in the gift certificate operating system.

The biggest problem comes when the business deposits gift certificate dollars as revenue rather than into a trust account. It should be classified as revenue only when it is redeemed. Within 6 months to 1 year, you need to pay staff and products on redemption. Some spas will only honor the gift certificate for 6 months; the redeemable period should not be more than 1 year, although certain situations may call for leniency.

The spa/salon industry is a personal service business, and customers are its bread and butter. They are sophisticated enough to realize that when they are told *"6 months is company policy because of accounting,"* the timeframe could actually be up to 1 year. Imagine customers being irate over purchasing a $400 gift certificate and finding out a spa/salon will not honor it because they were a month late in using that voucher. Remember that if you take care of your current customers, you will not need to spend thousands of dollars advertising for new ones. Research other successful operations that sell gift certificates, and check their gift-redeeming policies.

Insurance Claims

An insurance claim payment system for clients having massages is a wonderful aspect of caring customer service if you have all your forms designed and a system to record, track, and submit the claims to the company. Some spas will make the client pay, and then the client must seek their percentage of reimbursement themselves. The first system offers extended customer service.

Payroll/Compensation

Your payroll system can be done by your bookkeeper or by contracting a payroll service company. Someone still needs to monitor and figure out hours of work and commissions on services and sales, however. Get advice from your accountant on creating a simplified system. Decide on a scale; the spa/salon industry is accustomed to commissions.

Still looking for ideas on how to set up a system? Salon Business Strategies, a Connecticut-based organization geared toward providing business information and education for the spa/salon industry, offers a monthly publication full of tips and ideas. Their Web site at <www.strategiesmag.com> features a number of concepts covering areas such as skill-based pay programs, team-based incentives, cash-flow planning, client retention, and even a sample spreadsheet on how to calculate staff payroll.

When it comes to payroll and profit, the validity of arguments on both sides of the coin need to be addressed:

- We want a profitable business.
- We want our staff to be properly paid.

A lot of businesses start off an employee at $6 an hour or a 50 percent commission, whichever is greater. That wage is not very different from the average retail store worker. Spa/salons employees—such as hairstylists, aestheticians, and massage therapists—who start out at such low wages also face the staggering task of paying off student loans and other living expenses, while trying to get a toehold in the business. Workers in the spa/salon industry are the lowest paid employees in the economy when it comes to trade skills—that is, having some kind of education or prerequisites you need to land a job in the business in the first place. If your business offers a share-of-profits incentive with management, however, never scrimp on your policy and always honor your agreement. Always be honest when calculating an employee's share of profits; otherwise you could earn a reputation in the industry for skimming.

Some managers actually want an ownership share, so their efforts are rewarded on the basis of annual profits—and a share of long-term growth for goodwill and value, which accrues to the benefit of the business owners. Devise a strategy to give or sell specific employees some shares, while being wary of tax considerations for both parties. Profit-sharing works with younger employees; older, experienced employees want remuneration for a piece of the action.

Scheduling

Your hours of operation will depend on location and your personal philosophy. If your business is located in a large mall or hotel, you will need to comply with the parent structure's hours of operation policy, which are usually in place 7 days a week and with longer hours than spa/salons in more independent facilities. Scheduling systems for large staff can be tricky, especially if staff members get sick, leave on holidays, or quit. Create a system that outlines the scheduling policy so that current and new employees will understand the business' expectations and level of commitment.

You might want to consider a job-sharing approach in which, for example, two people share a chair in a salon that operates 7 days a week from 9 a.m. to 9 p.m. This system can work very effectively, with increased earnings for staff and business as a result.

Personnel System

Without people you have no business; remember the owner creates the organization and the organization creates business. Some owners are hands-on in the business, whereas others are absentee proprietors who hire salon managers and spa directors (who, by the way, are extremely hard to find). There are also a lot of wannabes, who know nothing about leadership, management, or the industry. My advice to absentee owners lucky enough to find a good manager or director is to appreciate their expertise and pay them what they are worth.

Although the spa/salon is rapidly growing, it is plagued by problems related to staffing. The Price Waterhouse Coopers 2000 Spa Industry Growth Study identified a number of specific personnel concerns:

1. Scarcity of qualified personnel and high staff turnover
2. Poor leadership and inexperienced management
3. Need for creative compensation programs and continuing education
4. Employees not capitalizing on the home-maintenance products that are necessary
5. Need to clarify spa industry language

The following information will provide insight and strategies on how to rectify those issues. To be a successful salon/spa owner you need to demonstrate *leadership*.

Leadership Development

Leadership is the ability to create a vision based on integrity, wisdom, and value for the human spirit and to effectively inspire and **coach** (to instruct, direct, or prompt) our team to achieve specified results.

"You cannot kindle a fire in any other heart until it is burning in your own."

Ralph Waldo Emerson

Leadership is developed from within when you do the following:

1. Know yourself.
2. Have vision, passion, clarity, and focus.
3. Understand human behavior.
4. Take risks.
5. Communicate effectively.
6. Show direction and create results.
7. Achieve results that benefit others, not just yourself.
8. Continually monitor progress through evaluation.

"Leadership is like beauty—it's hard to define but you know it when you see it."

Warren Bennis

A leader has power, electricity, magnetism, and presence—a drive that refuels, restores, and increases enthusiasm. Darryll S. Leiman, the spa director of the Aladdin Hotel in Las Vegas exemplifies leadership displayed by the passion and professionalism of the team he put together in this amazing and beautiful facility. A pleasant surprise awaits clients early in the morning when entering the spa facilities. The staff are awake, happy, courteous, excited, and very proud of their facility—stretching over 32,000 square feet with 35 private therapy rooms (including six multiple therapy suites for individuals and couples), a full-service hair and nail salon, and a gymnasium filled with cardiovascular and muscle-strengthening equipment. It is an awesome, state-of-the-art facility.

Besides the visual beauty, what amazed me was the caring and helpful staff. One employee, Naomi, pleasantly and enthusiastically guided me through the facility, explaining equipment and specific treatments and services they offered. She had me lie on a fantastic flotation bed purchased in Germany. It felt like a soft warm waterbed that expanded at the sides and cocooned me. When I finally met Darryll, I was impressed by his knowledge, experience, goals, and vision as well as his heart-and-soul approach to quality service.

His resumé reads like a world atlas, with post-secondary degrees earned in institutes in South Africa and Liverpool, where he graduated with a degree in exercise and physiology. Darryll got his first big break working at the 1984 Olympics Games in Los Angeles and wound up running the Spa at Sea program for the Golden Door, working on four world cruises. After spa stints in Italy and Hawaii, he landed a consulting job with the international chain Mandara Spa, where he set up a cruise division. Besides running Elemis Spa in Las Vegas, he still administers three cruise ship spa operations from his desk.

"I personally interview every new potential staff member and look for passion and fire, which can be molded and guided," says Darryll. "Challenges include keeping oneself balanced and healthy in this nurturing career," according to Darryll. "The key is knowing what services and treatments to create in this dynamically growing industry for well-educated consumers demand quality services and treatments in all aspects."

The Power of Change Masters

Throughout history, we have read about or personally know individuals who can walk into a room and cause energy shifts by their very presence. These individuals, called **Change Masters,** are truly themselves and speak their truth; not willing to just please others, they have found their authenticity. These individuals are brave and courageous because they have worked on themselves, developing profound insight from their conscious journey of direct experience.

They are not the intellectuals; they are individuals who know about life through the wisdom of their own personal *transformative* processes. They make incredible mentors and guides because they innately know and understand that the *magic of life* is about shedding the old and embracing the new. They *see* individuals and situations for what they truly are, as opposed to what they would like them to be. Knowledge may be clever, but it does not care. Wisdom, however, has the heart element of compassion.

Change Masters seem to flow through life, living with spirit and allowing others to "be." They meet you in the moment and see the bigger picture of circumstances. Unless you are prepared to consciously want the truth, do not ask a Change Master for advice. Some individuals actually shy away from Change Masters because they sense they can actually see their soul. Change Masters have been there, done that; they think for themselves and graciously walk their talk. Change Masters use their intuition when making choices and decisions. They believe in synchronicity, recognizing the divine source and plugging into that source through the conscious and subconscious mind that spreads your thoughts out into the universe.

We all see life differently. Some people think things out logically; others are highly intuitive. Some are good at mathematics and science, whereas others are natural artists or actors. A true leader knows herself/himself very well, understands human behavior, and uses the magical whole brain by combining the following:

- Logic and intuition
- Thoughts and feelings
- Past experience and future potential
- The practical and the visionary

Not all people desire to be leaders, and a leader's psychological maturity evolves when respecting and accepting differences in individuals.

A story Leo Buscaligia tells in his book *Love* is about a group of people who decided to set up a school board and develop a curriculum for the animals in the forest. In their wisdom, they decided all animals needed to learn core subjects such as flying, running, hopping, and climbing. They even set up an evaluation and grading system.

They were astounded during the first evaluation period; there were some unforeseen problems. The bird, excellent at flying, failed in running and climbing trees. The squirrel was a natural at climbing trees but flopped at flying. The rabbit scored top marks in hopping but did not make the grade in flying and climbing trees. More importantly, because of their frustrations and feelings of inadequacy over failing in other areas, they could not perform their innate skills as well as they could before.

Learning and the Instant Expert

True learning, which is the process of taking in knowledge, information, and facts, involves moving it to the understanding level, which can be fun and joyous. Learning to invest your time doing what you do best, and allowing others to do what they do best, will reap rewards.

There are many great **assessment tools** (instruments that identify individual differences in people) in the marketplace for understanding differences in human behavior and personality that can be used to increase productivity and employee morale. However, a lot of individuals administering and teaching the assessment tools need to be questioned on their credentials. People consider themselves experts after reading a textbook or taking a weekend workshop.

Industrial and organizational psychologists use an instrument called the Meyers-Briggs Type Indicator, a questionnaire that identifies individual differences. This particular instrument is based on Carl Jung's work, stressing that the way a person functions is far more important than understanding what motivates him. It has been an effective tool used in more than 2 million businesses across North America. Assessment tools are excellent to use in the recruiting process. The Meyers-Briggs Type Indicator and learning styles are assessment tools that are concerned with how a person takes in information and how he or she processes that information. As a leader you need to discern who can do what well and combine their talents into an effective team.

Studying human behavior helps us to know ourselves and gain an understanding of others: how we think, how we act, our beliefs, and our perspective on life. By identifying individual traits, we can choose to develop areas we are weak in to create a sense of greater balance. The more integrated you are as an individual, the more effective you are as a leader. Every organization needs a variety of talents: thinkers, communicators, doers, and support people. Just as in the forest—rabbits, squirrels, birds, etc.— everyone's skills and talents are necessary and are important.

Customers will relate to people with similar traits. For example, someone highly analytical will find it frustrating to work with someone highly expressive. When such incompatibilities occur, people will rattle off comments such as "We're on different wave lengths" or "We're not on the same page."

As a business owner you may want to invest in purchasing an assessment tool or contract that service out to a company who specializes in administering the assessments. Research the different assessment tools and personally try the ones available to see which one feels good to you, makes sense, and fits your business needs.

Top leaders demonstrate the ability to do the following:

- Raise awareness and show direction and guidance.
- Create intentional, deliberate results.
- Coach and inspire others to achieve their goals.
- Share achieved progress.

This type of leader creates results. When you are more confident, relaxed, and focused, you perform better. You tend to smile more and actually enjoy your work. Clear thinking or clarity allows you to be more effective under pressure. If the vision is clear, the passion comes.

Are you a true leader who has the ability to turn your vision into results, making it a win–win situation for all? Through a deeper understanding of human behavior, you can build a strong, healthy support team to share the success of your business. Attracting, training, and keeping staff is not only a challenge in the industry, it is a sign of the times. Changing times force us to face these challenges and be more innovative. A leader creates systems and procedures that support professionalism.

Most individuals live hectic lives just making ends meet. There are conflicts in relationships, and the traditional family support systems of the past have waned. As a leader, you need to create systems that create comfort and feel-good experiences, not chaos. Individuals start out with anticipation and excitement in a new job. So, what happens? Unless they know what is expected of them, what they are to do, and receive positive feedback about what they are doing, they will lose interest.

Remember, how you coach and treat your staff determines how they in turn treat the clients. True professionalism, the pursuit of excellence, not just skill competence, will create a quality, client service with higher profits. It is a leader's moral responsibility to invest in systems, supervision, and evaluation. Systems are designed with consequences (penalties) for noncompliance (failure to follow) with company policies. Set high standards in your organization.

You will also need a company policy manual to outline procedures, policies, and practices for all personnel within your business. Performance-based job descriptions, an employee contract, an application form, a procedures manual for services and treatments, employee performance evaluations, and a recruitment system are available as appendices at the back of the book.

Training/Education Program

Imagine your spa/salon with a team of individuals who are happy peak performers. Lasting and consistent peak performance is the result of individuals who are self-directed, know what the expectations are, and enjoy their work. Everywhere we hear or read about training or lifelong learning as a great investment in the business world. As with everything else, you need to discern what knowledge you desire and the instructional process to get it. Effective training programs increase individual understanding, comprehension, and retention and allow implementation of the knowledge presented. True understanding and implementation of knowledge are achieved only when the student is actively engaged in the learning process, instead of being a passive participant where information is simply presented.

Research and new discoveries are giving rise to changes in educational methods. "Most of us are in favor of improvement, as long as it doesn't include change," says Dr. Gary Phillips in his book, *Tools for Teaching for Transformation*. He shares tools and strategies for educators who recognize that teaching has moved from "informing to transforming." Education and training help employees advance their skills and attitudes, revitalize their methods, and apply new cutting-edge ideas. If you allow your organization to stagnate, you fall victim to more alert, progressive, and innovative competitors. Less than 1 percent of all the information the mind takes in actually reaches our awareness. *At least 95 percent of what a learner takes in is the experience, not the words.*

> *Tell me, I will forget.*
> *Show me, I will remember.*
> *Involve me, and I will learn.*

Teaching and training involves setting up the learning environment with meaningful learning materials that support experiential learning. Only through relationships to the whole does meaning arise—you cannot learn as effectively in isolation. To earn an education degree you need to attend university for at least 4 years. Even then, some teachers know the material but cannot transfer the acquired knowledge to the understanding level. As an owner, director, or manager, you need to seriously accept the responsibility for developing your team through education. Educate and develop yourself as a leader and coach by determining who will train your staff and understand what benefits your staff will derive from that information.

Sense when your staff and customers are becoming bored and listless. One of the pleasures of change and novelty comes from the heightening of attention—and the increase in brain activity it brings. The brain gets energized whenever something new or unusual comes along, getting more active as it perks up to pay attention. We delight in the new, whether it be a haircut, outfit, body treatment, traveling—even changing the furniture around.

Boredom is a symptom of low levels of attention.

A leader creates excitement and newness!

A lot of individuals take a weekend workshop on personality analysis or learning styles and think they are experts. In my experience, a little knowledge can be dangerous; problems that arise with the following *theory types:*

- Too easily stereotyping and trivializing human complexity (Yes, it can be fun, but some people take it very personally.)
- Often have static fixed ideas, which become self-fulfilling prophecies
- Too easily boxing individuals into a *pure* type

Roger Sperry won the Nobel Prize for his split-brain research by devising a theory that the left and right hemispheres of the human brain approach learning differently. Left-brain thinkers tend to be language- and math-oriented and are skilled problem solvers by processing information in a linear fashion. Right-brain thinkers are more artistic and graphic-oriented and are great at creativity, brainstorming, and daydreaming.

Recognizing these approaches, American theorist David Kolb discovered even deeper fundamentals to learning:

- Perceiving information and an experience is what we do first; some individuals think or reason, whereas others sense and feel.
- Processing information and an experience is what we do after we perceive; some watch and reflect, whereas others jump right in and do.

There is evidence that individual differences among people confirm that one cerebral hemisphere is more aroused than the other. Whole-brain learning may be accomplished for different people with different methods.

Connecting through Emotional Intelligence

Emotional intelligence, the act of making heart connections, is what we all desire as individuals. Once we have the skills, strategies, and wisdom to perform to our full potential, we excel. Personnel in the spa/salon industry touch peoples' hearts. Energy cardiology, which describes the energy of the heart, suggests you hum with your own frequency that combines information and energy. Beethoven's deafness forced him to tune into his *heart's* *code* rather than rely on his brain's sense of hearing. Our hearts want more than hectic living and chaos. Give your people a vision and invest wisely in their education. It may take up some of their valuable time; but the positive results will come back tenfold.

To develop an education and training program for your organization you need to do the following:

- Identify educational needs: skills, new information, and personal development.

- Develop programs and processes to contribute to the education and learning of the individual.

- Recognize the importance of organizing, planning, consistency, and repetition, which ensures quality and the future in education.

With planning and caring for your personnel you create the results:

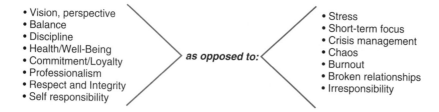

- Vision, perspective
- Balance
- Discipline
- Health/Well-Being
- Commitment/Loyalty
- Professionalism
- Respect and Integrity
- Self responsibility

as opposed to:

- Stress
- Short-term focus
- Crisis management
- Chaos
- Burnout
- Broken relationships
- Irresponsibility

Dr. Benjamin Bloom of the University of Chicago studied 100 extraordinary successful youth athletes, musicians, and students. He was surprised to find out the young prodigies did not start out by showing great flashes of brilliance. Instead most received careful *attention, guidance,* and *support* and then began to develop.

As a leader, you are a coach who provides direction and concentration for the players' energy by helping channel their energy and effort toward a single desired outcome.

Respect is earned. People have to see you doing things, time after time, that make sense to them in a larger way. They need to recognize that your actions are motivated not by your ego but by your desire for them to be the best they can be. *If you need to be popular when pushing people, your effectiveness goes and so does the respect.*

According to Don Shula, who led the Miami Dolphins to two Super Bowl victories and cowrote *Everyone's A Coach* with author Don Blanchard, coaching involves the following:

- Overcoming peoples' resistance and inertia

- Pushing people because they need to be pushed

- Not allowing sloppy practices and pushing the team to continually improve
- Having high expectations and confidence

Once the team becomes sloppy, it becomes a habit, and it is tough to get the team focused. Players thrive on pressure, when they know what they are supposed to do and how to do it.

Five-Step Plan for Coaching People

Follow this five-step plan for coaching people:

1. Tell people what you want them to do.
2. Show them what good performance looks like.
3. Let them do it.
4. Observe their performance.
5. Praise progress and/or redirect.

Staff working as a team create the synergy to perform and satisfy the customers. Great coliseums and facilities do not draw the crowds. The players do, and they create the great experience for the fans, similar to the great experiences in the spa/salon. Each player has practiced and trained to be the best; if they do not perform, they are cut. In nature, beautiful forests can be destroyed by one single diseased tree. Discern when to remove a staff member who does not respond to coaching/training and education. Your systems and procedures of education and training, aligned with a vision of professionalism, will create a winning team.

Someone who takes the team concept to heart is Don Grylls, who, with his wife, owns Manestreet Inc. and Hairsystems in Saskatoon, Saskatchewan, Canada. "Over the years I have spent considerable time reflecting on the dynamics of our industry," says Don, who hit the big time when he joined the Canadian Hair World Team 1998 for a competition in Dusseldorf, Germany, and has a talent for motivating his staff to get their customers looking and feeling great once they exit his salons.

"I have often contemplated the formulation that leads salons to celebrate long-term success stories for both their teams of beauty professionals and the clientele they attract. What is it that allows salons and spas to retain clients as return-requests—as opposed to having them seek services elsewhere?"

While preparing a presentation for the Master Judges Panel of Canada (a body that adjudicates cut and style competitions across the country), of which he is a lifetime achievement level member, Don came across his answer. It was a quote by American author Louis Nizer—who compared and contrasted the actions and attitudes of laborers, craftspersons, and artists—that got him thinking about the essence of team-building in his business.

A person who works with their hands is a laborer.

A person who works with their hands and their brain is a craftsperson.

 A person who works with their hands and their brain and their heart is an artist.

"I found this quotation particularly relevant and meaningful for all of us involved in the beauty industry," said Don, who also holds bachelor's degrees in education and fine arts.

"I felt that Nizer has encapsulated in words why some salons have in their possession that magical combination of elements to create client experiences which are in fact *golden experiences beyond their expectations.* Nizer's words act as indicators for answers to the question of differing levels of both excellence and longevity within our industry. Those of us who aspire to and achieve that combination of hard work, mastery of our craft and genuine caring and giving attitude are those who reach the highest levels of artistry in the services we provide for our public and continue to be some of the most influential persons in our communities across our country."

You might be able to change peoples' behavior. But if the heart and spirit are left out of your interactions you have not touched the inner essence of your people.

Marketing, Research, and Development Systems

Marketing includes everything used to sell and promote your services, products, and organization. Marketing, research, and development are all integrated because they all work together, and most small- to medium-size businesses do not have the budget to separate the departments.

Malcolm Gladwell, in his book *The Tipping Point,* revealed a phenomena that everyone seemed to agree was important but no one seemed to know how to define: the mystery of word-of-mouth. He describes three types of individuals: connectors, mavens, and salesmen. These individuals, he said, are distinguished not by worldly status and achievement but by the standing they have with their friends. People look up to them out of love because these kinds of personalities have the power to break the rising tide of isolation and immunity.

Augustus Belcourt, a dynamic hairdresser from Camrose, Alberta, Canada, touches the hearts and souls of his clients. "As a hairdresser for over 30 years I have had a unique opportunity to see the world before me in my salon," he says. "The thing that has been the most profound is the honesty that has been shared by the people who have come in for a service. My life could be said to be somewhat common except for the intimate contact I have had with my clients."

As his clients went through life changes such as divorce, separation from children, and other hardships, Augustus felt himself going through some of these darker passages. While working in his salon, he has met people who suggested workshops on personal growth and healing to deal with life's challenges. He eventually set up a reference library in his salon and has hosted monthly meditation sessions for the past 7 years.

"This journey has taken me to many places to heal my wounds and help me to grow," he says. "Today there is an authentic person in me that can be more loving, accepting and hopefully a guide to others inner authentic selves. Today I give back the acceptance I have been given. I love my clients, who may not know what they have done for me. Just the other day I was walking on the street doing an errand and had a kiss blown towards me from one corner, a hug on another corner and I thought to myself, 'Wow! How lucky I've been to be a hairdresser!'"

A woman named Sadler wanted to increase the knowledge and awareness of diabetes and breast cancer in an African American community in San Diego. Seminars in predominantly African American churches did not work for her, and she was determined to get the message out. She needed to find a place where women were relaxed, receptive to new ideas, and had the time and opportunity to hear something new. Her messenger needed to be someone who embodied all the traits of a connector, maven, and salesman.

Sadler deduced that women employed in salons work two to eight hours a day, depending on the service, and that a stylist had a special long-term and trusting relationship with the client. She was aware of instances when customers would drive 100 miles to see their favorite stylists—likely the same person who took care of them while they were going through life changes such as graduation, marriage, and children. Recognizing that stylists are natural conversationalists and very intuitive, Sadler got together with a number of stylists throughout the city and coached them on how to share the information on breast cancer. She then kept the stylists updated on new information; once her evaluation program concluded, the feedback was overwhelmingly positive.

She used no billboards, radio, or media. The power of word-of-mouth by the right people is more potent. Now consider how, through training, planning, and focusing that energy, you could market your business! People in the spa/salon industry are naturally doing *relationship-marketing,* usually for everyone else except themselves. Stylists let their clients know about the great sale at Store X, or the doctor they love, and yet they may not share information on the new color technique or the super massage therapist in the spa.

A dear friend of mine went to a spa for a facial and with hopes of purchasing a skin care line, having finished the product line she had been using. During her facial, she prompted the aesthetician 10 times, trying to get information on a skin care line. After her facial she was frustrated and disappointed that she had no home-maintenance products to take home. "Unbelievable," she said. "What do I need to do?" She also was interested in learning about mud and body treatments, but no one was interested enough to give her information.

So, owners, directors, and managers, before you spend thousands of dollars on billboards, radio, newspaper, trade shows, and other gimmicks, I suggest you spend some of those dollars effectively training and monitoring staff performance to take care of the clients you do have. Otherwise, you might eventually lose the customers you do have, or you may not be able to attract the ones you are trying to get through your advertising. They will eventually find a spa/salon that will fulfill their wants and desires. As an owner, you need to consider your clients' perceptions of your professionalism and your personal reputation. You cannot get the benefits of a reputation for truly outstanding customer service—or anything else—if you treat it as an occasional thing to be done. Intending to do something is worth nothing.

Most individuals lack the discipline to create structured programs to improve performance significantly. Do your market research and market analysis, design a marketing plan and marketing strategy, and train your staff. Identifying marketing tools and then planning your strategies within your budget begins the process. Through your research, you have targeted your specific market and appropriately chosen your services and treatments.

Everything Is Marketing

Certified Marketing Director Terry Willox is a 30-year, international, award-winning marketeer who has extensive experience in all aspects of the branding process, retail promotions, mall marketing, and promotional activities including special event planning and grand openings. If it needs professional marketing, presentation, and a bit of "let's put the *razz* back into ma-tazz," Terry, who is president and chief imagination officer of Whambhamram Marketing Solutions will get it done.

| *Figure 2-1* | Clean and tidy reception area. |

Terry has contributed the following insights: "One of the most misunderstood words in this business and many others is the word 'marketing,'" he says. "What does it mean to you? There are people out there in the world who, when they say they're going to 'do the marketing,' simply mean going shopping at the grocery store. It runs full circle from that understanding to those who fully understand it. Marketing to me as a long-time marketeer means many things as it relates to this business. It means in essence absolutely everything you do, say, show, treat, present, and carry on in your very specialized businesses."

Terry believes marketing touches on every aspect of business. "It's how you treat those very special people, your clients. It's all about properly maintaining exceptionally clean premises, creating long-lasting memorable visits on a regular basis, and how you go about ensuring they have those regular visits booked in advance. It's how you communicate with those clients while they're in your premises. Are the magazines up to date, are they greeted in any way or are they offered a cup of tea? It's about how staff is trained. It's how your products and services are presented on premises and in all communications (Fig. 2–1). It's about how the staff is 'upselling' your products and how they go about it. In short, "Everything is marketing. Don't you forget it. It's as simple as that!"

According to Terry, **branding** (a marketing process that identifies and positions your business in a very distinctive way in the marketplace) is one of the most important and integral components in marketing, promotions, and communications. "Because of the creative nature of this industry, the branding of a new concept is more of a process than just dreaming up a logo," he says. "It certainly isn't something that is created and tucked away; instead, it's a flowing unit that requires solid attention, refinement, and good management. Although the subtle distinctions of a brand can change over time with the marketplace pop culture and client turnover, the basic essence of the brand should live on. The process of creating a brand is a collaborative one, involving all concerned from the owners of the new concept to the creative team struck with this most important evolutionary process. There can be no schedule as to how long this process may take; it could evolve quickly or take time. Budgets and personal complexities or input may have a reflection on time spent on this type of process."

Terry suggests the first place to start on marketing is at the introductory "getting to know you phase," where information about the owners—from anecdotal tidbits and background to level of expertise and their competitive edge—is compiled. More discussion, concentrating on including artistic elements and concepts, takes place until a brand is created and approved. A "style book" is also developed, which indicates how the brand is to be used in print, TV, film, and other media as well as in all marketing materials, from brochures to promotions.

We will look at specific areas within which you will choose to focus your energies, from basic marketing materials and plans to more complex cross-marketing, as well as building strategic alliances and relationships (see box on page 44).

The list could go on and on. Get creative and innovative.

A lot of individuals who do not plan ahead say they want to be spontaneous. You need to plan a full year ahead, anticipate events, and use a variety of strategies. Almost every month has an event, including religious occasions, birthdays, and anniversaries. Some specific events or situations to consider are as follows:

1. Valentine's Day
2. Easter
3. Mother's Day
4. Father's Day
5. Secretary's Week
6. Wedding Season
7. Christmas
8. Graduation
9. Back to School
10. New Moms
11. Partner Getaways
12. Mom and Daughter specials

MARKETING STRATEGIES/TOOLS

1. Company logo
2. Company name
3. Business cards
4. Letterhead
5. Gift certificates
6. Signage
7. Service menu/brochure
8. Bags
9. Press release
10. Banner for trade show
11. Telephone, message, music
12. Promotional print to advertise on sign, print media, pictures, products, etc.
13. Web site
14. Loyalty card
15. Corporate packages
16. Spa/salon memberships
    - Business clubs
    - Community involvement
    - Charities
    - Sports teams
17. Trade shows
18. Promotions
19. Publicity
    - Radio
    - Television
    - Billboards
    - Print media
        Journals
        Newspapers
        Magazines
        Flyers
20. Education/information seminars
    - Lunch hour sessions
    - Evening sessions
    - Makeup classes
    - Experts
        Plastic surgeons
        Yoga instructors
        Herbalists

When you are planning your promotions for a specific event, packages sold as gift certificates work very well. Instead of discounting, give added value. Give a gift, such as a small size of a retail product you know they will love and purchase. (See the box on page 45 for examples.)

With Option A you lost $20.00. With Option B, the cost to you was $10.00 (maybe) and the client has a gift.

Setting up strategic alliances with other businesses to cross-market works extremely well. Joining a Chamber of Commerce and other business clubs lets you build relationships. Major sports teams, art, theatre, and music associations work well synergistically.

Get Virtual with the Web

A Web site is a must these days. Make sure you work with a company that you have researched and checked for excellent referrals.

"The role of a Web site in business is a medium for reinforcing brands," says Ken Bautista of Hotrocket Inc., a network of industry-leading marketing and technology companies that provide high-tech business solutions to a number of industries including petroleum, retail, governments, and arts organizations.

"Digital marketing using the Web is as critical as traditional marketing initiatives such as print and television. Effective digital media and marketing solutions help foster brand awareness, increase loyalty, and strengthen customer relationships through innovative, multi-channel digital campaigns. Whether it's a Web site, kiosk, e-mail campaign, broadcast animation, CD/DVD-ROM, streaming video, or interactive game, it is important to create unified, valuable, and engaging customer experiences that further reinforce and differentiate your brand."

Before selecting a consultant to help create your digital marketing campaign, Ken suggests you think about your business model and how your company makes money. He also suggests you identify key stakeholders and customers, your position in the industry budget, and the purpose of having a Web site.

"Having the answers to these questions will provide your web consultant with a better understanding of your business and your industry, which allows them to formulate a much more effective and focused digital marketing strategy using the Web," says Ken.

On-line booking is effective but can be complex and expensive. If you are large enough to warrant a call center, make sure you understand the complexity and cost.

Research, develop, and evolve to stay in tune with the trends. Demographically driven market shifts have important implications that require careful consideration for any company in this intensely expanding and competitive spa/salon industry. Visit other spas in person, experience treatments, and visit their Web sites. Subscribing to excellent publications in the industry allows you to keep abreast. Attending conventions and joining associations allows you the opportunity to acquire the knowledge and skills that are essential to staying abreast of change in the competitive and constantly evolving beauty industry.

Have fun exploring *newness*. Your staff and clients want the best; **be a leader in the industry.** Remember that your staff is following your lead. Keep them excited and enthusiastic.

Option A

$200 package—discount 10% = $180

OR

Option B

Give a gift, such as body lotion. Your cost would be $10. Make a deal with the manufacturer to buy "X" amount and get a certain amount free of charge.

Concepts for Consideration

1. How would a business benefit from knowing the challenges, changes, and trends in the spa/salon industry?
2. What approach would you use to develop a marketing plan?
3. Describe how leadership skills benefit you as an individual and a business organization.
4. What are the values and benefits of knowing and understanding the variable and fixed costs of services and products?
5. How would you develop a plan for coaching individuals?

CHAPTER 3

Spa/Salon Development and Design

If you are a spa/salon business owner and are thinking of expanding, or if you want to build or purchase such a facility, clarify your vision and develop a plan of action. The design of your spa/salon will depend on a variety of factors:

- Spa philosophy
- Vision
- Budget
- Theme
- Location
- Square footage of space
- Demographics
- Future area of growth
- Per capita income
- Competition

My experiences have revealed that individuals interested in the expanding spa/salon market have diverse and varied backgrounds. From these backgrounds evolve different perceptions of what a spa/salon really is.

The eclectic backgrounds of these individuals may include the following:

- Hairstylists, salon owners
- Aestheticians, massage therapists, cosmetologists
- Alternative health care practitioners, healers
- Medical doctors, plastic surgeons
- Fitness and wellness practitioners
- Professional business people, such as lawyers, accountants, entre-preneurs, realtors, retreat owners, hotel and resort owners

People deciding to be a part of the spa and/or salon market niche have personal agendas. After interviewing a number of individuals about why they entered into the business, I uncovered a list of specific reasons:

- It is a good business opportunity and a good investment.
- It is an excellent tax write-off.
- They had the desire to expand services for existing clientele.
- They were interested in well-being, health, and youthfulness with definite alternative healing philosophies.
- They had a love of working with people (nurturing service indus-try) and helping people look and feel good.
- They felt excited about being a part of such a high-growth, inno-vative market.
- They had a love of expression in the fashion, artistic, and beauty areas (glamorous, exciting, and trendy).

Although we all have our own perceptions of what spas and salons are, some fundamental elements of this market niche need clarification. Not only are consumers confused with the array of types of spas and treat-ments, I see many owners, managers, and directors of such businesses ex-pressing confused, fragmented, and foggy ideas. Some business owners be-lieve offering aesthetic services such as pedicures, manicures, and facials qualifies them to advertise their facility as a spa. In my experience they are an *aesthetic studio/salon* or *mini-spa*.

Individuals may encounter positive and negative experiences when visit-ing a spa for the first time. Positive experiences entice the individual to return to the same spa or experience other spas while traveling. Negative experi-ences tend to sour an individual's perception of what a spa is. My experience of visiting a spa that had great print advertisement in the phone book was shocking. To reach the "spa" you had to journey through a dirty salon area. The "spa" was one room with a green door where body treatments, facials, and massages were performed with no sink or shower.

The Power of Words and Perception

Some basic definitions and terms are needed to clarify aspects and fundamentals relevant to this market. Moving from a historical perspective and experiencing the spa and salon evolution, we will discover the true essence of this incredible market niche.

The term **salon** was first used during the Age of Reason, sometimes called The Age of Enlightenment (1687–1789), when intellectuals believed that the use of logic could be applied to improving the way people lived and were governed. Back then these salons actually were the homes of several women who opened their abodes to writers, artists, poets, and essayists of both sexes to discuss freely their ideas, which contributed to the Age of Reason. It was not beauty that distinguished the salons, but a combination of intelligence, grace, influence, and unobtrusive money that enabled the hostess to make the gathering sparkle with wit or wisdom.

Today clients choose to visit salons for more than beauty treatments. Some go for acceptance, social enjoyment, and lively and fun discussions, among other attractions (Fig. 3–1).

Roman baths were a popular gathering place.	*Figure 3–1*

The term **spa** originates from the Roman Empire, when soldiers went to hot baths and pools to heal their ailments and wounds. *Sanus per aquam* (spa) has its meaning defined in health, through or by water. Spas, developed throughout Europe, used mineral water, seawater, and marine substances combined with body therapies. My perception is that a hydrotherapy component is the basis for discerning and defining spa facilities. Kneipp, a German priest who lived from 1827 to 1897, developed water treatment to cure illnesses. In Europe, the acknowledged national health cure is defined as preventative health care, based on the acceptance and use of spa therapies. Medical doctors studying to be spa doctors incorporate the modalities of balneology, natural therapies, thalassotherapy, climatology, and other disciplines into their studies.

Spa Concept

To create and build the spa, we need to determine the spa concept based on a particular spa philosophy, individual needs, desires, vision, and budget. You will need to define the type of facilities you envision, location of facilities, specific services and treatments, and equipment and products.

One person who came up with a unique spa concept was Surinder Bains, owner of the Miraj Hammam Spa in Vancouver, British Columbia, Canada. Surinder was born and raised in Victoria, B.C., before moving to Vancouver to complete a degree at the University of British Columbia. She owned and managed a highly successful travel agency in North Vancouver that allowed her to travel the world extensively. In 1986 she packed her bags and moved to Paris where she met and married her husband. Surinder first visited a **hammam** (Arabic for *"spreader of warmth,"* a method of cleansing with steam without bathing) in Paris at the suggestion of her husband. On entering the hammam, she was immediately overwhelmed by how different it was from a European spa.

"I had such an emotional release and realized I had been introduced to something that made me very aware of a complete comfort of my body and soul unlike anything I had ever experienced," she said.

After years of thorough enjoyment, Surinder passionately desired to introduce this tradition to Canada by opening her spa in Vancouver so that others could share in the experience. Her goal was to successfully combine this aspect of Islam refinement by marrying it harmoniously into the North American environment and marketplace.

Indeed, a hammam is drenched in many ancient traditions. In 600 A.D., the Islamic Prophet Mohammed endorsed the hammam (the steam) as a method of cleansing without bathing. Another tradition has it that mothers would frequent hammams in search of future brides for their sons. The hammam was and still is a place where women can comfortably socialize in a spiritual and healing environment. It is regarded as a necessity, and if a woman's husband forbade her to go to the hammam, it created grounds for divorce.

Traditionally, women and men had separate chambers in hammams, hence the Miraj Hammam Spa offers separate women's and men's days. Miraj Hammam Spa is the very first hammam in Canada and is located in Vancouver's prestigious South Granville area, noted for its art galleries, antique shops, and exclusive retail stores. Both the exterior and interior of Miraj have been distinctively designed to reflect the Middle Eastern heritage from which this concept arose.

The exterior entrance features wrought-iron grillwork, gates, and a canopy. Wooden double doors carved with Persian archways provide entry into the reception area, resplendent with tiled floors, columns, arched passageways, curved ceilings, replica Moroccan lamps, and a trickling fountain set in mosaic tile design—all finished in warm colors. The sanctuary and heart of Miraj features the hammam, a shower/change room, three massage rooms, and the Sultana Lounge—all with Middle Eastern music playing in the background.

After taking a quick shower and donning a sarong, clients enter the hammam chambers. These consist of a low-mist steam and intense steam chamber, complete with Jerusalem gold marble slabs on which to repose and a very large marble fountain in the center of the room. After spending time in the two steam areas, a *gommage* (a full scrub with authentic black Moroccan soap) is applied to the body. The very best natural oil-based products are used in the gommage, massage, and facial chambers. Following the gommage treatment, a robe is provided for clients to continue on to a massage, to a facial, or directly to the Sultana Lounge. In the lounge, a leisurely rest on an expansive velvet lounge with silk cushions and servings of Middle Eastern tea and sweet cakes concludes this unique experience.

Surinder commutes between Vancouver and Paris, maintaining a home in both cities. After 4 years of extensive planning, determination, and development Surinder created her dream Miraj Hammam Spa. That is what *passion* and *focused vision* can do. Visit Surinder's Web site <www.mirajhammam.com> to discover this unique experience.

Types of Spas

The following spa designations will help you clarify your vision of the type of facility you desire to develop and build.

Day Spa

A day spa is a facility with or without a beauty salon and/or fitness component. It can be owner managed or multi-chain operated and located in hotels, resorts, retreats, malls, or freestanding buildings. Spa experiences are created with specific treatments in certain timeframes. Half-day or full-day packages are available, hence the term "day spa."

Destination Spa

Destination spas usually thrive in warm climates with beaches, oceans, mountains, or deserts. They are more extensive in the spa experiences with a longer timeframe, such as 5 to 14 days. Clients usually desire a more holistic approach to their well-being with a more physical, philosophic, and spiritual component. Accommodations usually include meals (specific to the spa concept), body treatments, fitness facilities, exercise classes, specific programs, medical evaluations, and outdoor activities. Pools, thermal waters, and sea water are available.

Resort Spa

The resort spa is an amenity available to guests at a resort setting. The facilities are sometimes separate from the resort, or they are incorporated with the resort facility. The resort spas usually are in resort areas and hotels in specific destinations, usually a warm climate. Individuals can purchase different packages; some are included with accommodations and meals service, and others are à la carte.

Medical Spas

A medical spa is a specific classification that may be designed in a day spa, destination spa, or resort spa setting. Usually they include on-staff medical doctors, plastic surgeons, dermatologists, and/or naturopaths who will perform health examinations or different forms of cosmetic and laser surgery. Medical spas are classified as the next generation of the spa industry. The International Spa Association defines it as an institution whose primary purpose is to provide comprehensive medical and wellness care in an environment that integrates spa services with conventional and complementary therapies and treatments. Plastic surgeons and dermatologists have been joining day spas and expanding their practices, offering higher level spa services and care. Pharmaceutical companies are designing products solely for medical spas. Hospitals and health insurance companies are even taking new steps in recognizing alternative medical care and coverage.

Fitness/Health Clubs

Fitness/health clubs are integrating spas into their facilities to expand well-being treatments to their existing loyal clientele. This is a great meld, if they can design the space to separate the two modalities. Excellent sound-proofing would be required to alleviate the noise from the hustle and bustle of traffic and individuals exercising.

Hospital and Rehabilitation Centers

Hospitals and rehabilitation centers have been offering physical therapy, water therapy, and specialized exercise programs. With the health benefits of spa treatments we are seeing more treatments and services being made available to patients.

Wellness Centers

Wellness centers—which have naturopaths and chiropractors; offer yoga, Pilates, personal development seminars, and weight-loss clinics; and sell homeopathic, vitamin, mineral, and nutritional supplements—are now jumping on the bandwagon and offering spa services and treatments. They also tend to have a good selection of retail items for well-being such as spa products, books, videos, and other health and wellness aids.

Spa Team-Building and Strategic Alliances

Now that we have clarified some of the fundamental terms related to the spa and salon market, we will look at the actual development and building process. Usually, at this point, serious business owners have their strategic alliances or team specialists in place.

The specialist team will consist of the following:

- Spa/salon consultant (designer)
- Commercial real estate agent
- Real estate lawyer
- Accountant
- Architect
- General contractor (specific subtrades)
- Manufacturers and distributors in the industry

Creating this specialist team involves a process of building relationships with individuals and companies based on respect, trust, integrity, and expertise in defined areas of interest. The old saying, "Sometimes, you cannot see the forest for the trees," certainly rings true when it comes to this aspect of specialist team building. Ownership has a huge component of "emotionalism" assigned to it. That passion is usually the energy used to create, but, with the excitement of this passion, certain required elements or qualities may be missed. Most of the time, individuals with specific expertise can see things and advise from a more detached but knowledgeable point of view.

There is no right or wrong; psychological maturity lets you respect differences in individuals. The most important element is to achieve the desired results through clarification of vision and discernment of the appropriate steps in development of the project. Everyone believes her or his personal perception to be the truth. It has been my experience that *the ability to develop a more creative, innovative experience of excellence is achieved by looking at a project from a more holistic point of view with a larger perspective, which is created when you have strong strategic alliances with experts in the particular field.*

Location, Location, Lease

Some individual clients choose a specific region, then a facility location, based on **demographics,** which are the statistical characteristics of a human population, and market surveys. Destination and resort spas have self-determining factors: climate and location. In many cases, clients are simply expanding their existing facility. Whatever scenario you are looking at, the following information is important when developing, purchasing, or expanding in the spa/salon marketplace. Location, personal vision, philosophy, and budget will all be important factors in the decisions that will affect your spa/salon business. Whether you are purchasing or leasing space, you will need to consider the viability of the location. Analyzing the location is just as important as analyzing the lease options.

Research very carefully your basic lease options because your lease affects the success of your spa and/or salon. Before signing your lease, have your commercial real estate agent or leasing consultant, your real estate attorney, and your accountant go through it in detail.

You need your team of specialists to help you with the following:

- Project construction and operation costs
- Forecast expenses and revenues
- Summarize square footage construction cost, rent, and amortization
- Customize profit-and-loss reports, return on investment, and break-even analysis, which are an invariable part of location and lease processes

At the same time another team of specialists is advising on equipment and product needs and designing the following:

- The facility—spa/salon reception/retail regarding space needs
- Treatment rooms
- The facility as to theme, color, textures, flooring, decor, lighting, and style of furniture and furnishing, to create ambiance.

Basic Location Types

There are three basic location types for salon/spas: regional malls, strip malls, and freestanding structures.

1. *Regional malls* usually have well-established spas and/or salons with owners who have substantial working capital. Large numbers of shoppers are attracted to the mall, which has adequate parking. The drawback or challenge is usually the cost of rent. The mall management company usually calculates the rent by the square foot, up to a break-even point, and then by the square foot or a percentage of your gross revenue, whichever is greater. Management usually adds on *common area maintenance* (CAM) charges, which can range from a few dollars per square foot to as high as $60 to $70 per square foot. CAM charges are often included in triple net lease payments, which include taxes, insurance, outdoor lighting, parking lot insurance, property taxes, snow removal, and sometimes utilities. You need to know in your revenue projections that you will gross a lot of money per square foot. The larger malls are tougher to negotiate with.

2. *Strip malls* are usually more affordable than regional malls, and the potential for expansion is often greater.

3. *Freestanding structures* are usually privately owned, allowing more flexibility and negotiation opportunity than other locations.

Spa and/or salon owners often are drawn to older structures because of the design, charm, and mystique. Restoration of these older buildings can be extremely costly with surprising challenges in the renovation process. Older homes (which may not be zoned) or buildings usually will require new plumbing, wiring, ventilation, heating, code upgrades, and structural refits. Make sure to check the foundation, structural tresses that support the roof, and the condition of the roof and eaves troughs.

Specific terms of real estate leasing and development, quoted directly from the Center for Commercial Real Estate, will help you in the following areas:

- Lease agreement
- Graduated lease
- Triple net lease
- Renewal option
- Base rent
- Escalation clause
- Lease commencement date
- Net lease
- Effective rent
- Concessions
- Leasehold improvements
- Tenant improvements
- Parking ratio
- Rental concession
- Abatement
- Space plan
- Design/build
- Turn key project
- Work letter—concessions
- Construction management
- General contractor
- Working drawings
- Contract drawings
- Building code
- Building standards
- Subcontractor (electrical, plumbing, mechanical, sheet metal, HVAC [heating, ventilation, and air conditioning] system, flooring, painters, mill workers, drywallers, fire protection, sprinkler system, signage)
- Economic feasibility

The most challenging aspect is the terms of the lease. Recommendations include a 5-year lease with options for renewal or a 10- to 15-year lease. Some owners claim it takes up to 3 years to really make money; be very shrewd when it comes to negotiating the time element of the lease. Sometimes a long lease, 10 to 15 years with an option, can allow more free initial rent, tenant improvement dollars, and/or a lower rent. Your negotiating power will depend on your ability to understand the entire leasing process and your ability to ask for specifics—in other words, the process of *"cutting the deal."* The landlord will not offer you special concessions. You may negotiate a noncompetition clause (exclusivity) and advance notification of property sale. When negotiating the exclusivity clause, write out the terms to prohibit the landlord from leasing adjacent or neighboring locations to businesses that derive more than 20 percent of revenue from competing products and services.

Compare the amounts of money you expect to make per square foot with the amount you will pay for rent to ensure profit in the location. Check the rent increase language in the lease; it is usually adjusted to the Consumer Price Index and can hit you with an unexpected rent hike. Try to negotiate fixing the price for the lease duration; then a fair rental increase would be 5 percent to 7 percent to follow the inflation rate.

Some landlords charge a percentage of your gross revenue, anywhere from 6 percent to 12 percent after your business has cleared a specified profit. In the spa/salon business, you may counter the gross percentage rate by explaining that this is a service business that thrives on lower gross profit yields than retail businesses. Try to raise the break-even point to where the percentage kicks in, which will save you hundreds of thousands of dollars over the lease term. If you are lucky, some landlords pay for water, which is a bonus in this business. Landlords will make allowances to businesses they perceive as long-term and stable. You may ask for several months of *free rent during construction,* which will save more business capital for your startup costs. Negotiate parking and signage yourself, and then have your attorney read the fine print and counsel you on the more significant issues.

Tenant improvement (TI) *money* is key when building in a new location or expanding an existing one. TI can range from an average of $25 a square foot to $125 a square foot. Many landlords will offer rent credit in lieu of TI money, but rent credit is cheaper for the landlord. If you choose the rent credit, negotiate an increase in the amount of rent credit offered. Tenant improvement dollars are used for expenses such as new wall construction, ceilings, doors, flooring, plumbing, and electrical. Utility equipment is not part of the TI money; landlords should pick up the cost on large utility equipment because it is their responsibility to bring utilities to the space. Some owners negotiate wherein the landlord pays for the HVAC system and the spa/salon pays for the smaller ducting costs. You should insist the landlord pay for the necessary code upgrades and check the transformers to see if they can handle the load. There are major challenges and frustrations when transformers blow. Clothes dryer ventilation can also become a costly item if you have to duct a distance and core through the roof.

"You don't get what you deserve. You get what you negotiate," says Jai Prusad, chief executive officer with Enokhok Development Corp., Ltd. Have your leasing agent and attorney help you clarify and understand your lease before you sign.

What the client, who is building the spa/salon, needs is a budget breakdown per square foot for financing and lease negotiation. This is the multitasking process that involves all the team members of your strategic alliances. You may opt to be your own general contractor or project manager if you have the expertise and experience. Have all your contracts drawn up and checked by your lawyer, so when you negotiate with your team specialists and subtrades, you are ready. A basic format for a contract, which you can modify, is available in the appendices at the back of the book.

Transforming Space through Design

When someone enters a spa/salon, their eyes and senses are activated and they make a decision about the facility based on *how they feel*. When merging or integrating a spa and salon in one facility you need architectural expertise in blending the two opposing energies: calmness and excitement. Marc Speir, president of the Allied Beauty Association, summed it up precisely: "The difference is a salon is rock 'n' roll and a spa is Enya."

It absolutely amazes me how many individuals perceive themselves to be architects and interior designers when it comes to designing, creating a theme, and decorating a spa/salon. Creating an aura of enchantment through a palette of sage, terra cotta, butternut, cinnibar–browns, beiges, combinations of or tone on tone of each has the senses react. Consistency in design, placement of lighting scones, and colors of walls can create a fluidity of movement and perception of a larger area. Fountains; fireplaces; real plants; herb gardens integrated with textured surfaces; and swirling silken, sheer, soft drapes can create pictures in your mind, even as you read. Designing the interior according to the Chinese art, **feng shui** (the Chinese art of placement based on an instinctive and learned understanding of relationships in space), or using curved walls can inspire harmony; earth tones can soothe the eyes and calm the mind.

"When designing a spa or salon, one of the most important realities is to consider how it will look and feel to the clientele. Obviously, the more positive and supportive the environment, the higher the probability of success and long-term sustainability created by a loyal and happy customer base. Feng Shui, or the Chinese art of placement, is a wonderful and readily available tool which can help ensure that the experience of the client is a direct reflection of the owner's energetic intentions. Through the informed use of color, shape, sound, light, water, and furniture placement, you can manifest a balanced and supportive work place. It is recommended that a certified consultant be hired to act as your expert guide in establishing good **chi** *(or energy, life force, vibes.) He or she can inform you of the nine different aspects of life and where those energies are maintained inside your physical space. Fountains, windchimes, different floor plans, plants–both natural and silk, artwork, hardware, and much more, can all play an important role on the type of success the owners achieve and the experience of the client."*

janetmayfield@shaw.ca

Chaotic homes filled with many disagreeing voices have been transformed into harmonious, peaceful environments, where a strong sense of tranquility prevails. This is what you want in a spa—an opportunity to allow your client to feel complete on all levels, giving them a great sense of satisfaction and money well spent, hence word-of-mouth advertising and return business. Let their spa experience touch the spiritual, mystical, or magical part inside of them, and you will have a loyal client base.

Feng shui, as a creative art and specific science, can be an excellent source of progress for all aspects of your business, from returning clients, to profits, to popularity and a united staff.

Consultants are not called architects but are known as experts. As with any investment you make, be sure to do your research. Ask about the consultant's training and years of experience, check some references, and discuss the cost before you set the date for the consultation. You can find listings of local consultants in alternative newspapers, at some specialty or gift shops, through Chinese medicinal practitioners, or on the Web.

A *seasoned architect*, with industry expertise and tradeskill, will work with an owner and get a sense of what it is you want to express in the spa/salon area space. Your image can successfully brand you. **Branding** (a marketing process that identifies and positions your business in a very distinctive way in the marketplace) is a powerful competitive tool because it conveys as much about your company values and principles as it does about your product or service.

AREAS TO CONSIDER

Areas to consider when analyzing and planning the available space are as follows:

- Signage
- Reception area
- Lounge area
- Coat check area
- Locker area
- Bathrooms/showers
- Laundry facilities
- Staff room
- Office
- Dispensary and stock room
- Steam facilities
- Sauna
- Pedicure area
- Manicure area
- Makeup area
- Styling area

- Technical/shampoo area
- Exercise room
- Meditation area
- Corporate meeting room
- Pool area
- Treatment rooms
- Multipurpose rooms

  Facial

  Massage

  Couples room

  Wet room

  Hydrotherapy room

  Specialized treatment room (men's and ladies areas may be separate)

There are some elaborate specialties that can be offered in the spa and may be developed if you have the space and the budget.

Watsu

Watsu is water shiatsu that is performed in a pool and is based on Zen Shiatsu, which is a relaxing aquatic movement therapy that emphasizes stretching the body. Warm water is an ideal medium for mobilizing the *chi* through the meridians. This holistic bodywork experience allows the client to be held close by the therapist, which has clinically proven benefits for the client. Physical therapists, massage therapists, and other body worker practitioners worldwide use it for the following:

- Reducing stress and anxiety
- Decreasing muscle guarding and tension

- Decreasing pain and fatigue
- Increasing energy
- Increasing range of motion
- Increasing circulation
- Improving breathing patterns
- Normalizing tone
- Improving body awareness
- Improving sleep patterns
- Stimulating the lymphatic system to release toxins
- Discovering and releasing emotional stress

Rasul

Rasul is an ancient Middle Eastern ritual that takes place in an ornately tiled steam room, which allows for the self-application of medicinal muds and a rain shower rinse. The Canyon Ranch Spa Club at the Venetian in Las Vegas, NV, is a 60,000-square foot health and fitness oasis. While touring the facility, I was fascinated with the Rasul Chamber, a self-contained, domed room with heated floors and seats. Every surface is covered with ornate, handmade tiles. The ceiling features showerheads, providing a natural-feeling rainfall and fiber optics so your experience seems to take place under a starry sky.

You embark on an ancient Middle Eastern ritual of Rasul, which takes place in this exotic, ornately tiled steam room. This cleansing ceremony includes self-application of medicinal mud, intermittent steam with herbs, and a rain shower rinse. This treatment is a prelude to an aromatherapy massage or moisturizing body cocoon that is perfect for couples—a very intimate and sensual experience. See Figure 3–2 for an example of a Rasul.

Labyrinth

As early as 4,000 years ago, the power of the labyrinth symbol was well recognized. Labyrinths are unicursal with 7 or 11 circuits with one well-defined path leading to the center and then back out. "The labyrinth is an archetype of wholeness that helps us to rediscover the depths of our souls," according to Dr. Lauren Artress in her book, *Walking a Sacred Path*. Please visit <www.gracecathedral.org> for more information (Fig. 3–3).

As spas take on their new roles as vehicles for healing and well-being, mental, spiritual, physical, and emotional services expand to meet all these needs. The original Golden Door Spa in Escondido, California, has a labyrinth outdoors to teach guests meditation. Patients undergoing chemotherapy and even physicians at the California Pacific Medical Center,

| *Figure 3–2* | A Rasul designed and built by Spavisions. |

an acute-care hospital in San Francisco, silently walk the outdoor concrete labyrinth.

A good-sized labyrinth is about 36 to 40 feet in diameter and based on sacred geometry, so the construction of it is very important. They can be built indoors and are popular throughout the world. An 18-inch square

| A seven-circuit labyrinth. | *Figure 3-3* |

labyrinth on a wall at the cathedral in Lucca, Italy, dates from the ninth century. People would trace the labyrinth with their fingers and quiet their minds before entering the sacred space. There are finger labyrinths available today that could be used while a client is sitting in a quiet room before or after a service or treatment.

Meditation Room/Area

The Phoenician Spa in Scottsdale, Arizona, has a unique and absolutely gorgeous meditation room. If you have the space you can create a sacred space for your clients to meditate. **Meditation** is a process of quieting the mind, gaining access to our inner wisdom and compassion, and resolving our inner conflicts in the process. By concentrating on your breath or a specific mantra, you can shut down the inner dialogue. You will know the power and ecstasy of silence when you *fall silent,* the most sacred place of all. A lot of individuals are practicing some form of meditation to relieve stress and increase their well-being. Transcendental meditation has scientific documentation as to the health benefits for individuals, such as lowering blood pressure.

You have a tremendous amount of options to design your sacred space into an extraordinary and profitable business with the right team of experts assisting you to create your dream. I know an incredible architect

WORDS THAT WILL ACTIVATE YOUR SENSES

The following list of words will activate your senses as to specific feelings created:

grace	sanctuary	calm	energy
elegance	oasis	timeless	exquisite
luxury	serene	bliss	spirit
fluidity	flair	sand	quiet
sensual	sophistication	sun	soft
esoteric	comfort	cozy	pamper
ethereal	warmth	fire	relax
youthful	splash	earth	clouds
fun	trickle	water	air
joy	flow	charm	eclectic
ambiance	rhythm	circular	caress
sensory	harmony	strong	smooth
oval	balance	light	shiny
round	feminine	dark	red
curved	ancient motifs	shadow	orange
luxurious	mystical	sweet	yellow
chiffon	frequency	blue	green
cotton	brocade	exotic	violet
pink	wind		

See what appeals to you the most when you think about your future spa or salon.

who builds a relationship with his client to the extent that he can create exactly what the owner wants. The architect then uses his expertise and knowledge of what is in style to create your personal expression of the space. The artistic architect integrates the artistic, scientific, and personal elements and creates through intuition—bringing forth into reality through the manifestation of thought forms, ideas, and images a unique theme for the space.

Traveling, reading, visiting, going on the Web, and personally experiencing different spa/salons allows you to *see* and *feel* all the possibilities. A beautiful room or spa/salon is a *work of art*. It requires a skilled hand, a perceptive eye, and the experience to know what works and what does not work. Every room must be composed with the utmost attention to detail, colors, texture, pattern, lines, and period style. Creating the experience in the mind and senses sets the stage for the spa/salon experience.

Here is a very good investment: find an artistic architect and experienced spa consultant to assist you in *creating your dream*. It is well worth it.

Concepts for Consideration

1. What are the benefits of identifying the factors that determine the design of your spa/salon?
2. How would a good leasing agent be of benefit to an individual wanting to open a business?
3. Why would you want to have strategic alliances or team specialists assist you in building your spa/salon?
4. How would clarifying the term *spa* and identifying the different types of spas be of benefit and importance?
5. How would identifying and understanding the challenges of integrating a spa into a salon assist an individual?

CHAPTER 4

Spa/Salon Equipment and Supplies

In deciding on the equipment you desire for your facility, you should be aware of everything that is available along with the fundamental equipment necessary to open a salon or spa. Your vision of the facility, as well as your budget, will determine what type of equipment you purchase. There are many excellent companies that can help you determine what you need. Once you know what is available, you will be able to research the specific benefits and values of particular equipment.

We each have our own perceptions; it is hoped that the following information will help you gain a wider perspective when researching and choosing your equipment. You will have a greater understanding of the types of equipment and be able to ask individuals helping you more relevant questions.

The Salon Area—Equipment and Supplies

Basically, the salon area will revolve around the stylist—the number of styling chairs and the design concept of the stylist stations and area will be determined by the design specialist working with you. Because we are an *image industry*, it is shocking that certain owners end up re-covering old stylist chairs, thinking a new color or fabric is sufficient. Line, design, form, color, fashion, and beauty are the basis of our industry. The new concepts

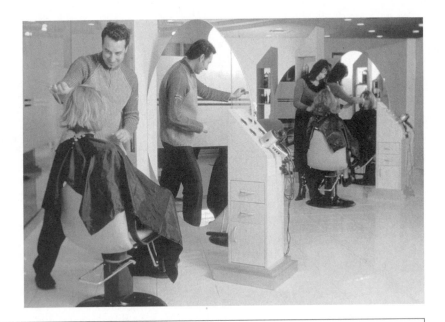

| Figure 4–1 | Spasation salon area. |

in salon furniture are also more streamlined and high-tech; they are less cumbersome than the older styles. You will achieve a cleaner, more fashionable image with the beautiful new designs in furniture. Your stylists and clients deserve the best (Fig. 4–1).

Styling Chairs

Some basic considerations when purchasing stylists chairs are as follows:

1. **Comfort/style:** Does the back of the chair offer good support, and will a large person fit in the chair comfortably?
2. **Cleanability:** Will the hair fall through to the floor, or will it get caught in the creases of the chair?
3. **Color and fabric:** Will it create a specific mood, enhance your theme, and make a specific statement, and is the fabric durable and easily cleaned?
4. **Durability of the hydraulic:** What type of guarantee and company support do you have?
5. **Functional:** Is the base of the chair easily cleaned and designed so it will not scratch the flooring when moved?

You as an owner will benefit from using the expertise of specialists in the industry. They can help you decide what salon furniture will provide the most advanced ergonomic and fashionable equipment for your stylists and clients.

Styling Stations

The stylist station with mirrors is your next consideration. Will the mirrors be freestanding or against the wall? You can purchase some of the beautiful prebuilt stations or custom design your own with help from design experts through beauty furniture industry manufacturers or with beauty industry distributors who work with specific manufacturers. Experts in the field can help you choose the specific material for your stations—wood, metal, etc.—to complement your salon theme. You need to consider if you want lighting integrated into the stylist station or specific overhead lighting for each station. The stylist station becomes an integral part of the overall design and part of available working space of the salon.

Some individuals who chose to design their own styling stations because they thought they would save money encountered challenges. For instance, one owner worked with a mill worker (who was not knowledgeable about the industry's needs) to design and custom build styling stations; major problems occurred because of their lack of expertise. Some stations were too bulky and looked homemade; electrical outlets were incorrectly hooked up; the building materials were inferior (the wood was so soft that it marked and stained easily); and, one of the most crucial elements, the reception structure was not ready. *Delays can be very costly if you do not open on the prescheduled date.*

Sinks

You will find different options when it comes to shampoo sinks. Consider your space and design of sinks before you make your decision. Different design concepts abound, such as the sink at the wall or the sink that allows you to stand behind it to shampoo the client. There are fabulous new concepts with the shampoo chair built as a part of the freestanding sink unit. The design of the shampoo chair is important for the comfort of the client. Personally experience how comfortable they are by sitting in them with an awareness of how they would suit the different postures of your clients. How would they feel sitting in them? You might want to consider a darker color for the fabric so color stains will not show. Consider the style of the shampoo sink (new shapes are very interesting), the type of material it is made of, the color, and the taps and sprayer. Many hoses on the sprayers crack and leak.

Dryers/Accelerator Machines

Will you be using dryers or the new accelerator machines for your hair treatments and services? Again, the new equipment tends to be more streamlined and fashionable. Consider the space each piece of equipment requires. Always remember that each square foot of area of the salon is costing you money and needs to effectively generate revenue, just as hours of operation need to generate revenue. The accelerator machines are faster, giving the stylist and owner more revenue-generating time by providing your client quicker service. Instead of processing a color for 30 to 45 minutes, the client is complete in 9 to 12 minutes (depending on the machine). Nowadays, everyone values their time, so customers like the new technology. If you do not provide these new experiences, they will find a salon that does.

Computer

A computer and software package specific to our industry is extremely important. Take your time when purchasing your computer and software package. Check with your accountant about the advantages of leasing your computer as opposed to purchasing it. Milano Systems offers a software program that is user-friendly with an excellent support system, which is an important aspect of such a program. More than 700 salons and spas across North America currently use this program. Research this and several other programs before making a decision.

Laundry

Most salons will be doing their laundry in-house as opposed to using a laundry service. You cannot afford to cut costs with washers and dryers. Commercial equipment is the best way to go; it might be more costly upfront, but it saves on repairs and stress when the equipment is not working. One client who purchased regular appliances rather than what was available commercially found out the warranty did not apply because they were being used in a business. Depending on the facility location (main floor or upper level), you need to meet certain specifications when considering washers and dryers. Consider things such as ventilation, hookups, gas or electric, and any restrictions that may apply in certain building codes.

The Aesthetic Area—Equipment and Supplies

The aesthetic area includes facials, waxing, manicures (hand therapy), pedicures (foot therapy), eyebrow and eyelash tinting, and makeup. Check with local health regulations regarding specific requirements for your

BASIC CHECKLIST FOR SALON EQUIPMENT AND SUPPLIES

For your reference, when planning your salon, keep in mind the basic checklist for salon equipment and supplies:

- Stylist chairs (for stylist area and technical service area)
- Stylist stations/mirrors/lighting
- Shampoo chairs/sinks (rubber neck rest)
- Children's booster seat
- Dryers, accelerators
- Computer and software package for reception area
- Washer/dryer
- Reception area furniture
- Music system
- Office furniture
- Filing cabinets
- Computer and software package for the office
- Fax machine
- Phone system
- Banking and credit card machines
- Vacuum system
- Antifatigue floor mats
- Trolleys
- Cutting stools
- Towels (shampoo/color)
- Shampoo and service capes
- Client gowns
- Stylist and client magazines and magazines holders
- Hair color lines: semi-permanent, permanent, high-lift, bleach, funky bowls, brushes, applicators, gloves, color remover, foiling, weaving, chunking materials
- Permanent waves: assorted sizes of rods, perm papers, cotton, neck trays
- Rollers: magnetic, clips, Velcro, hot roller sets
- Specific retail and professional back bar shampoos, conditioners, treatments, and styling aids
- Decorative items: pictures, mirrors, tables, plants, flowers, candles, etc.

services; some require a sink in the room for certain services. You would also want a commercial washer and dryer specifically for aesthetic laundry; you need to keep in mind the same considerations discussed in the section on salon area material.

Although the aesthetic equipment is not highly visible, except in private treatment rooms, you still need to remember the *image* aspect when deciding on your furniture. This information will be given in a different format for the specific service.

Facial Lounge

Your aesthetic lounge will be the fundamental piece of equipment for performing facials. The knowledge and expertise of spa/salon equipment manufacturers and distributors will help you make wise decisions when purchasing your lounge, considering the incredible assortment of lounges to choose from. Being aware of the many types of lounges available allows you to do your own research. I always suggest experiencing the equipment by actually laying on the lounge to *get the feel*. There are basic to deluxe models of aesthetic lounges. You can get them in different sizes and shapes and with hydraulic lift, single pedestal, split leg, integrated lumbar, electric, and multipositional features. Just like salon furniture, the lounges have become more streamlined and less cumbersome. Before designing your treatment rooms, make sure you have decided on your aesthetic lounges because of

SOME BASIC CONSIDERATIONS

Some basic considerations when purchasing aesthetic lounges include the following:

1. **Comfort/style:** Is should be ergonomically designed for client comfort with integrated lumbar support. The rounded contour as opposed to the square form embraces **feng shui** (the art of placement that is based on and instinctive and learned understanding of relationships in space).

2. **Multipositioning:** It allows ease when positioning client.

3. **Hydraulic system/electric lift:** It allows the therapist to position the client. Check the ease of using the hydraulic system, and check how smooth and quiet the electric lift is.

4. **Upholstery:** The upholstery should be high quality, easy to maintain, and fire resistant.

5. **Base:** The base should be stable yet not so bulky as to cause the stylist to hit his or her feet on it.

6. **Side arms:** Some lounges have swivel arms for ease of lying on the bed and for specific treatment needs.

the different sizes. Once, a client creating a spa brought me in after the treatment rooms were built. When discussing his equipment needs, I realized he was unaware that lounges came in different sizes; he assumed they were standardized. We happened to be on-site and I took out my measuring tape to measure the treatment room. It was far too small, even for a small lounge. Two options surfaced: position the lounge horizontally in the room—which would cut down on working area for the therapist and other needed essentials in the room—or start tearing down walls.

Facial Machine

A facial machine or skin care unit will depend on your philosophy about machines, budget, training level of staff, and what particular professional skin care line you have chosen for facials. Most units will have a steamer and magnifying lamp with a light. Options, depending on the specific facial machine, would include the following:

- High frequency
- Vacuum spray
- Rotary brush
- Iontophoresis
- Woods lamp
- Suction
- Sprayer

When purchasing a facial machine or skin care unit, make sure your staff will use all the options, or purchase a very basic unit. I have seen a number of machines just sitting in a room not being used—which is money invested but having no return.

Instead of having a facial machine or skin care unit in each facial room, you can be creative and offer specific facial treatments in specified rooms. A facial steamer may be purchased separately from the facial machine or skin care unit. A steamer that produces **ozone** (a bluish gaseous reactive form of oxygen that is formed naturally in the atmosphere and is used for disinfecting, deodorizing, and bleaching; pure and refreshing air) and one that has an integrated system for using essential oils are good investments.

Magnifying Lamp

A magnifying lamp with a light is an essential piece of equipment for each facial room. When purchasing the unit, be sure to check if it is a three- or five-diopter lens or the five- and seven-diopter double magnifying lens. They now have a great unit that includes a steamer and magnifying lamp combined with a light. There are also skin scanner systems using "black light" to analyze the skin and determine specific treatments.

Microdermabrasion

With new technology come the **microdermabrasion** machines that introduce a new method of skin rejuvenation and refining lines. There are many different machines to fit your particular needs. Personally experience the treatment so you have an in-depth understanding of the process. It is a large investment, so make sure your aestheticians believe in the treatment and are trained so they can sell the service.

Dynatronics Corporation produces a machine that offers microdermabrasion and cellulite treatments through delivering deep, subdermal tissue massage for treating typical cellulite problem areas such as hips, thighs, buttocks, and abdomen; it is great for lymphatic drainage. My experience with the revolutionary vacuum massage technology, which is proven to enhance the appearance of the skin while increasing circulation, was very powerful. To purchase some machines, there may be a mandatory hands-on training program for certification.

Waxing Area—Equipment and Supplies

The decision to create specific waxing treatment rooms, or to combine the service area within other treatment rooms, will depend on the number of treatment rooms in your facility and your needs. If you decide to have specific waxing treatment rooms, your basic aesthetic lounge without the side arms will be the fundamental piece of equipment you require. Check the recommendations stated in the facial area section for lounge specifications. A lounge without side arms allows more ease and closer proximity to the client when performing body area waxing services. A magnifying lamp with a light positioned behind the head area of the lounge gives the therapist more focus and clarity when performing facial waxing services.

There are numerous wax pot heater systems. Check your local health board regulatory specifications when it comes to the roll-on type waxing systems; they are unacceptable with certain health boards. Over the last few years more concerns have surfaced about skin being torn while waxing—not just facial skin, but body skin as well. Price point is important, but not when it compromises quality of service or customer safety.

Manicure (Hand Therapy) Area— Equipment and Supplies

There is a large selection of tables that will fit into the theme or style of your salon or spa. Some tables are very basic; others are high-end with specialized options. Consider your budget and area space.

BASIC CHECKLIST FOR FACIAL EQUIPMENT AND SUPPLIES

For your reference when planning your facial area, keep in mind the basic checklist for facial equipment and supplies:

- Aesthetic lounges
- Aesthetic stools
- Facial machine/skin care unit
- Facial steamer
- Magnifying lamp with light
- Skin scanner system
- Microdermabrasion machine
- Face and body toning unit
- Portable trolleys
- Sterilizer
- Hot towel cabinets
- Hydrocollator
- Bowls (assorted sizes)
- Containers for gauze, eye pads, cotton, compresses, cotton strips, cotton swabs, spatulas, brushes, sponges
- Gibson towels
- Thermal blankets
- Sheets/pillowcases
- Pillows/bolsters
- Towels (assorted sizes)
- Lambswool table pad
- Table warming pad
- Headbands
- Robes/slippers
- Cover-ups
- Garbage containers
- Laundry hamper
- 70 percent alcohol and sprayer bottles
- Antiseptic hand cleaner
- Distilled water
- Witch hazel
- Essential oils
- Cleansers
- Toners
- Masks
- Scrubs
- Eye creams
- Tonics
- Serums
- Moisturizers
- Massage creams
- Disposable lancets

Specialized options available include the following:

- Drawers
- Light
- Hand rest
- Product area
- Mini-vacuum system

A good support stool with a back and excellent lighting is important for the manicurist, whereas a comfortable chair is vital for clients.

BASIC CHECKLIST FOR WAXING EQUIPMENT AND SUPPLIES

For your reference when planning your waxing area, keep in mind the basic checklist for waxing equipment and supplies:

- Aesthetic lounge
- Trolley
- Magnifying lamp with light
- Wax pot heater (single or double)
- Wax
- 70 percent alcohol and sprayer bottle
- Disposable paper/paper holder
- Robes/slippers
- Disposable panties
- Gibson towels
- Towels
- Antiseptic hand cleanser
- Antiseptic cleaner/witch hazel

- Baby powder
- Hair retardant/antigrowth serum
- Medicated soothing lotion
- Wax cleanser
- Body/facial tweezers
- Wooden and metal spatulas
- Epilation strips (assorted sizes), muslin strips (assorted sizes)
- Gauze
- Orange wood sticks
- Essential oils
- Paper for the lounge
- Laundry hamper
- Garbage container

Do your research on the many different nail systems for sculpting or tipping nails and always keep in mind the educational support and price point. Take precautions with systems using a drill because not all nail technicians have the sensitivity to work with drills. Nail technicians will have their own preference for a specific system. These practitioners move around a lot. Always remember that if you want support, education, and special deals, you need to build a loyal and trusting relationship with your nail supplier.

Pedicure (Foot Therapy) Area—Equipment and Supplies

There are many styles and concepts in design available for pedicure equipment, depending on the design of your facility. Will the pedicure unit be portable so you can move it to certain areas, or will you have a specific pedicure area? Choosing the portable pedicure unit alleviates the additional plumbing or necessary installation. Success in the industry requires owners to offer more than *basic services*. With more deluxe units you can build *distinction* in services, which will guarantee greater market share, profitability, and growth. You may purchase or custom design and build deluxe pedicure units.

BASIC CHECKLIST FOR MANICURE EQUIPMENT AND SUPPLIES

For your reference when planning your manicure area, keep in mind the basic checklist for manicure equipment and supplies:

- Manicure table/light
- Manicurist stool and client chair
- Therabath for paraffin treatments
- Mitts and plastic bags for paraffin treatment
- Nail systems equipment (lights) and products
- Finger bowls
- Containers for gauze, cotton balls, cotton swabs, orange wood sticks, emery boards, nail brushes, sandstone, buffers, cuticle nippers, pushers, nail clippers
- Gibson towels
- Towels (assorted sizes)
- 70 percent alcohol and sprayer bottle
- Antiseptic hand cleanser
- Nail polish remover
- Nail polish remover dispenser
- Soak for the nails
- Muds/masks/exfoliators (specialized treatments)
- Massage oils
- Cuticle oil, cuticle remover
- Small applicator bottles if purchasing cuticle oil/cuticle remover in bulk
- Base coat, top coat, nail strengthener, nail dry
- Nail polish (assorted colors); seasonal fashion colors, matte, shiny, funky, glitter
- Nail art supplies (depending on fashion/trend)

Some units have built-in manicure tables that capitalize on saving time for the client. The deluxe pedicure units offer such options as the following:

- Whirlpool
- Massage chair with heat
- CD player
- Multipositional chair
- Adjustable foot rests

Figure 4–2   Spasation pedicure treatment room.

- Adjustable seat swivels and slides to accommodate different client heights
- Plumbing accessibility (make sure your plumbing specifications adhere to local plumbing codes)
- Available lighting when performing services

You may decide to custom design and build your own pedicure units depending on area space and personal needs. Building specific pedicure treatment rooms with as many pedicure stations as you desire—and having as much individual privacy for clients—calls for creativity and innovation in your overall facility design (Fig. 4–2).

Eyelash/Eyebrow Tinting Area—Equipment and Supplies

The aesthetic lounge and lighting recommendations for the eyelash/eyebrow tinting area are similar to requirements for the waxing area. You may want to have specific treatment rooms for waxing and eyelash/eyebrow tinting depending on the facility design and personal needs.

BASIC CHECKLIST FOR PEDICURE EQUIPMENT AND SUPPLIES

For your reference when planning your pedicure area, keep in mind the basic checklist for pedicure equipment and supplies:

- Pedicure unit lighting
- Therapist stools with good back support
- Therabath for paraffin treatments
- Booties and plastic bags for paraffin treatment
- Paraffin wax (assorted scents)
- Robes/slippers
- Towels (assorted sizes)
- 70 percent alcohol and sprayer bottle
- Polish remover
- Polish remover dispensers
- Disposable gloves
- Antiseptic hand cleanser
- Containers for cotton balls, cotton swabs, toe spacers
- Cuticle oil/cuticle remover
- Small applicator bottles if purchasing cuticle oil/cuticle remover in bulk
- Foot soak
- Muds/masks/exfoliators (specialized treatments)
- Liniments
- Callous and corn remover product
- Base coat, top coat, nail dry
- Nail polish colors (assorted—same criteria as for manicures)
- Massage cream/oil
- Moisturizing lotion
- Products for dry, cracked skin
- Fungus treatments
- Powders
- Professional line for cabinet area and retail line for home maintenance program
- Paddles
- Drills
- Credo/pediknife/blades; check your state/provincial regulations
- Emery boards
- Nail brushes
- Large nail clippers
- Cuticle nippers/cuticle pushers/Hindu stones
- Buffing blocks
- Metal scoops
- Laundry hamper
- Garbage container

Makeup Area—Equipment and Supplies

When designing the facility, decide on where you want your makeup area. Your design team will help you make this decision, taking into consideration facility size and personal needs. Visit some large department or specialty stores and analyze their cosmetic and makeup areas. Spend some time watching client flow, space allotted for makeup application, design

BASIC CHECKLIST FOR EYELASH/EYEBROW TINTING EQUIPMENT AND SUPPLIES

For your reference when planning the eyelash/eyebrow tinting area, keep in mind the basic checklist for eyelash/eyebrow tinting equipment and supplies:

- Basic aesthetic lounge
- Magnifying lamp with light
- Containers for cotton balls, cotton swabs, gauze, applicators, brushes
- Bowls/containers for color and water
- Black/light-colored towels (assorted sizes)
- Antiseptic hand cleanser
- Paper shields

- 70 percent alcohol and spray bottle
- Eyelash/eyebrow colors (assorted)
- Eyelash/eyebrow developer
- Eye area cleanser (water-based)
- Oil-based protective eye cream
- Eye cream
- Skin tonic (sensitive)
- Laundry hamper
- Garbage container

and type of equipment, how they work with their clients, and how many clients they service in a particular timeframe. It is also informative to see how they operate and the numbers of sales generated. Deciding on a particular makeup line will take some research: quality of the makeup, price point, and how extensive the line is are some major concerns to consider. You may decide on a makeup line that customizes foundation colors, or you may decide to have your own labeled company name brand.

There are many styles and material specific brushes (sable, goat, etc.), which determine the prices.

- Makeup in assorted fashion colors and skin type

  Foundations: water-based, oil-based, liquid, crème, compact, etc.

  Concealers: cover cream/stick for corrective makeup

  Blushes

  Lipsticks: matte, shiny

  Eyeliners: liquid, pencil

  Lip gloss

  Lip liners

  Shading powders

  Translucent powder

  Shimmer

  Mascara

BASIC CHECKLIST FOR MAKEUP EQUIPMENT AND SUPPLIES

For your reference when planning your makeup area, keep in mind the basic checklist for makeup equipment and supplies:

- Makeup table/lighting
- Storage unit
- Stool for client
- Mirror
- Makeup cape
- 70 percent alcohol and bottle sprayer
- Makeup brush cleanser
- Antiseptic hand cleaner
- Hand-band/clips
- Containers for custom blending foundation
- Palette for working product
- Cleanser, toner, eye makeup remover, moisturizer

- Containers for sponges, disposable mascara applicators, cotton swabs, cotton balls, gauze, spatulas, eye shadow applicators
- Tweezers
- Makeup brushes
  Powder
  Blusher
  Contour
  Eyeshadow
  Eyeliner
  Brow
  Eye lash
  Lip

- Eyelash curler (have client bring their own in)
- Artificial eyelashes/adhesive
- Laundry hamper
- Garbage container

The Spa Area—Equipment and Supplies

The individual spa owner's vision and philosophy of the concept of *spa* can serve as a guide to research all types of spa equipment and understand all the benefits and values of each piece of equipment. There are basic to trendy pieces of equipment available, which can be very costly. Research particular types of treatments and services you would like to have in the spa by experiencing the different treatments, services, and equipment yourself. With practical experience, you can analyze the specific pros and cons of the available options.

While experiencing the services, treatments, and equipment, always keep in mind the feeling you experience: Was it awesome or just okay? Was it relaxing and comfortable? What benefits and value did you receive from it? How user-friendly was the equipment, and what was involved in the clean up? Always remember that the staff needs to be trained. You want a simple, effective, unique, and joyous system to create an unforgettable healing experience.

Consider, when deciding on how to outfit your facility, what treatments and services you can offer with each piece of equipment. You need to take into account the actual total costs of the equipment—allowing for variables such as renovations, installation, and monthly costs for lease or loan payments. Figure out how many services and treatments you have to perform over a determined time period before you realize a return on investment. Can you be creative and innovative with designing new services and treatments? Many business owners have become disillusioned with their equipment because of breakdowns, maintenance, installation, staff uninterested in promoting the service, inexperience with treatment or service procedures, and marketing the treatment or service. Spend time researching and analyzing your equipment needs because equipment is a large investment.

The spa industry in North America is in a youthful stage compared to its European counterpart, and we are learning a lot through research, experience, and shared information. Some owners have created beautiful spa facilities with specific treatment rooms and incredible equipment that is either not being used to its full potential or not being used at all. Identifying your personal equipment needs will be based on spa philosophy, facility design budget, and services and treatments offered.

Steam facilities: Your choice of a steam room, canopy steam, or steam cabinet.

Steam room: Do you want co-ed or separate rooms for males and females? When designing and building your steam rooms, it is imperative you consult with experts in the field. You need to consider size, design, materials, steam units, steam doors, and labor involved. While designing your own steam rooms, be diligent in researching the steam doors and the steam generator system. In my experience these two areas presented major challenges such as steam leakage through the doors and generator breakdowns.

Steam canopy: A portable steam therapy system that will increase muscle suppleness and create a deep sense of relaxation as your client lies on the massage table. A simple steam generator sits on the floor at the foot of the massage table and connects to the canopy; no plumbing is required. The canopy is lightweight and easy to lift—you can either have an area in the treatment room to store it or hang it from the ceiling with a specially designed pulley system. It is a small investment when compared to the steam room; again, personal needs and philosophy are considered.

Steam cabinet: A portable steam therapy system with wheels that makes transportation easy. Some units offer adjustable seat height, and there is no plumbing required.

Showers: Will you design and build the shower or purchase the unit showers available on the market? Facility design and theme have a lot to do with this decision. Make sure you are aware of the building codes in your particular area (especially with handicap access) and health board regulations. Check to make sure the shower accessories and taps are easy for clients and staff to use. We tend to overlook these small items, which can be very frustrating and costly.

Massage tables: It has been my experience that massages performed on certain tables were uncomfortable because the tables were too small. According to massage textbooks for training massage therapists, the dimensions should be approximately 28 or 29 inches wide and 76 inches long. Most massage tables are 4 to 8 inches shorter. Make sure you have your table dimensions before designing the treatment room. A well-designed massage table allows the therapist to move about, or change positions, without breaking the rhythm of the massage movements. You also need to be able to adjust the height of the massage table, depending on your therapist's height.

Check the construction of the table to make sure it does not shake, rock, or squeak. Some tables have a height-adjustment button and are operated by hydraulic force or electricity; although costly, they are useful for the elderly and disabled. A face cradle and armrests are a must. Some massage tables are constructed from wood with a storage area beneath; some are all metal, whereas others are a combination of metal and wood. Make sure the padding is thick enough for comfort and the fabric is durable and will not stain. Always buy your equipment from a reputable company that guarantees its products. You may want to consider some innovative new dry flotation massage beds or mermaid hydrotherapy tables. There are specific massage systems that lay flat on the floor for *shiatsu, Thai,* and other massage therapies.

There are many different types of bolsters and cushions designed to optimize prone, supine, and lateral positioning. They can even accommodate pregnant clients, women with large breasts, and men with large stomachs.

For the client who may opt for a mini-back massage instead, a portable massage chair is a must. It is a very effective piece of equipment, when used correctly, as a marketing tool for speaking engagements and health and wellness or trade shows. Choose from several types available in the marketplace. Variables you need to assess include comfort, angle adjustments (so you can control spinal alignment and cervical flexion), and positioning capabilities that give extra strength and leverage with less back

BASIC CHECKLIST FOR MASSAGE EQUIPMENT AND SUPPLIES

When planning your massage area, keep in mind the basic checklist for massage equipment and supplies:

- Massage tables
- Therapist stools
- Portable massage chairs
- Floor massage systems
- Bolsters and cushions (assorted sizes)
- Anatomic charts/posters on the muscular system, skeletal system, Chakra system, trigger points, meridians
- Robes/slippers
- Towels (assorted sizes)
- Table warming pads; optional
- Fleece pads
- Sheets: top and fitted bottom
- Blankets
- Pillows
- Face cradles
- Heat therapy units to keep gels, oils, lotions, and creams just above body temperature; optional
- Containers for oils, lotions, and creams

- Hot towel cabinets
- Hot packs, heating pads, thermal/heat packs
- Power massagers; optional
- Antiseptic hand cream
- 70 percent alcohol and sprayer bottle
- Massage oil: There are many different types. Some will go rancid easily and some will stain your sheets. Mineral oils are not recommended for massage. They are a petroleum-based product and have a tendency to dry the skin and clog the pores.
- Liniments for hot and cold therapies
- Essential oils (of a high quality to be mixed with a carrier oil, unless doing raindrop therapy)
- Gems (gem therapy)
- Stones (stone therapy) and stone heaters
- Laundry hamper
- Garbage container

strain for the therapist. Many portable massage chairs sit in storage areas because of missing screws or defective parts. Your investment is not bringing in any returns while in storage, and it is frustrating and time-consuming to call in a repairman or have it taken out for repairs.

Hydrotherapy Treatment

Hydrotherapy includes equipment using the science of water treatments for external applications to the body.

- **Balneotherapy:** water therapy that uses fresh water
- **Thalassotherapy:** water therapy that uses sea water and products from the sea
- **Thermal therapy:** water therapy that uses hot spring water

The man who developed water treatment as a means of curing illness, Sebastian Kneipp, was a German priest who lived from 1827 to 1897. According to Reinhard Bergel, PhD, the International Kneipp Association, a nonprofit organization with its head office in Munich, has developed a network of treatment sanatoriums throughout Germany, Austria, Switzerland, Luxembourg, France, and southwest Africa. Medical doctors who have taken special training in the Kneipp Cure privately own most of these clinics.

Hydrotherapy offers many powerful and health-enhancing treatments if performed correctly and to its fullest potential. Many designs and types of hydrotherapy tubs exist in the marketplace from very basic models to very deluxe versions. Choosing a specific tub for your facility will take some research and some collaboration with specialists in the field. Many reputable manufacturers and distributors have a wide selection of different models of tubs. Whatever your philosophy, knowledge and understanding of hydrotherapy tub treatments, services, and experiences will definitely affect your choice of tub. You should experience some hydrotherapy services with different tubs. Staff education on the value and benefits of treatments and procedures is imperative (Fig. 4–3).

In my experience some spas have exclusive hydrotherapy treatment rooms with incredible equipment not being used. For the most part, staff do not like cleaning the tubs and tend to leave clients alone in the room when they could be performing a wand massage or a head, neck, and/or scalp massage. It is extremely sad when such state-of-the-art equipment is gathering dust when there are incredible benefits that could be realized by the client. Some questions to ponder and keep in mind when researching and shopping around before making your final decision are on page 87.

Vichy Shower

According to Andrea Sercu of *Day Spa* magazine, the **Vichy shower** (a water therapy treatment that incorporates a multijet rainbar that is suspended over a wet bed/table and used in special treatments to bring the body into balance) goes back to the 1800s, when patients who had manic depression or schizophrenia would journey to the hot springs of Vichy, France. Under a small hole drilled in a simple pipe, they sought the calming elixir of the earth's warm, lithium-based mineral waters.

Figure 4-3   Spasation hydrotherapy tub for specialized treatments.

Today, clients wish to experience therapeutic benefits from modern Vichy showers that have controlled water flow, temperature, and pressure. Do your research when deciding to have a Vichy treatment room; you are looking at the cost of the equipment as well as the expense of the wet room. Purchasing your Vichy shower may depend on the room design and plumbing needs. Before purchasing your Vichy shower, do your research and talk to manufacturers, distributors, and spa consultants. Seek out expertise from individuals not connected to a particular company, and experience the different systems personally.

Personal experiences with Vichy showers will give you a lot of insight. In my experience, as I lay on the wet table, the room was cold and I felt exposed, and there was no savory scent or aroma in the air. The water temperature fluctuated, and my therapist was not enjoying this experience because she was getting wet. The therapist was having difficulty adjusting the showerheads to have the water focus on specific body areas because of the height of the bar. When she stopped the shower, drips of water continued. Rather than feeling calm and serene, I was agitated about all the little nuances. It was not the incredible, sensual rainfall I had dreamed of experiencing.

DECIDING ON HYDROTHERAPY EQUIPMENT

■ What is my budget and what market niche will I want to attract, considering my facility, location, and demographic information?

■ What size of tub do I require (there are oversized tubs for large, less agile clients and the extra room will allow for underwater wand massage), and how will I position the tub in the treatment room?

■ Do I want the massage wand for specific treatments?

■ Do I want a water jet system, an air jet system, or a combination of both?

■ How many jets and what types of jets do I want? How will the jets be positioned in the tub?

Water jets spray water, whereas air jets spray air; the water jets work on the body and the air jets move the water, oxygenating it.

The underwater jets can be arranged in six independent anatomic circuits for individual treatment of ankles, knees, thighs, buttocks, waist, abdomen, spinal column, and feet.

Do I want a special oxygenating system built in the design of the tub?

■ Does the tub have handrails and a sprayer, or is that extra?

■ Does the water pump have a large capacity, and is it "whisper" quiet?

■ Are the plumbing and electrical components approved by code in my specific demographic area?

■ Do I have a large enough electrical breaker and a ground fault?

■ Is there an integral cleaning/disinfecting cycle? Is it manual or automatic?

(Some tubs have a continuous ozone disinfecting system.)

Do I require a temperature gauge, timer, and/or music?

Do I want a highly computerized system for specific programmed treatments?

Do I want the lighting system that allows automatic action of brilliant colors? Should it have single color or continuous change?

Do I want a reverse-osmosis or other filter system to remove the **chlorine** (a nonmetallic element that is found alone as a strong-smelling, greenish–yellow irritating gas that is used as a bleach, oxidizing agent, and disinfectant) from the water so it does not interfere with the process involved in the specific treatment?

Do I want an ozone option, which further purifies the water in a natural way, producing an energized feeling from enhanced oxygen levels?

Do I want to purchase a tub that has the option of putting a top on it to convert it to a full-size massage table and wet treatment center? If the answer is yes, take into consideration the height you want the tub to be to offer the extra treatments so the therapist is not bending down. (Dry hydrotherapy allows a client to float comfortably fully clothed on a dry hydromassage bed that combines invigorating massage, soothing warmth, and full-body flotation, without getting wet.)

Facilities that move a client from room to room disturb the healing process of the body. Compare the room-to-room experience with an option called the Integrated Spa System, in which the entire treatment is done in one dry room. The canopy was placed over a special massage table, which allowed me to stay warm and have more privacy. Rather than have to move from room to room, all treatments were performed on the one table. My experience included an aromatherapy steam, then a relaxing massage, followed by a remineralizing body treatment. Once the treatment was applied, the canopy was placed back on the massage table to allow for another steam, which helped the penetration of the treatment ingredients. When the desired treatment time was complete, the canopy with the Vichy shower built into it was used. As they used the wand technique on me, it felt like a gentle rainfall over the body. Finally, a moisturizing treatment was applied to my body—a heavenly experience.

"Hospitals offering alternative health treatments is a growing trend in the medical community with a greater focus on prevention and optimal performance in health. Decatur Memorial Hospital, in Decatur, IL, has created a state-of-the-art wellness facility, which offers the Integrated Spa System. This system which allows steam, massage, wet table, and Vichy shower treatments is part of the wellness centre offering the best hydrotherapy and massage treatments," according to Richard Edison, owner and designer of the system (Fig. 4–4).

Figure 4–4   Integrated Spa System—steam, massage, wet table, and Vichy shower.

More and more unique Vichy shower systems are making a splash in the marketplace today. You can choose from many models of wet tables; usually the individual companies that have them will recommend the Vichy system. With the hydrokinetic Vichy shower packages, you can choose your wet table, which comes with options such as pedestal or stationary bases and contour or fold-down tables. You may choose the size of your rainbar; obviously it will depend on the table length you decide on. The hydrobonnet option will help to keep the therapist dry.

DECIDING ON A VICHY SYSTEM

Some considerations and questions to ponder and keep in mind when researching and shopping around, before making your final decision are as follows:

■ What type of customer service can I expect from the company I purchase my Vichy system from? One owner had to wait 4 months for a Vichy system ordered from France. However, I can recall excellent service from several different companies. When deciding on a Vichy system, phone a spa that has the system and ask about customer service and support. Spa owners are often friendly and accommodating when offering advice; they also let you know if there are any particular problem areas with the system.

■ What kind of hands-on-training can I expect my staff to receive? Staff needs to be confident in the procedure and believe in the value of the service.

■ How will the client feel exposed on the table?

■ Will I encounter problems of excess water, cold clients, and soaked therapists?

■ Will there be accidental drips when the shower is turned off?

■ Will there be surges in water temperature, or is there a safety shutoff valve?

■ Will I find a system where I can easily focus the showerheads to a particular body zone, and can I have a fine mist and a focused pulsating force?

■ Can I have a system that can change the condition of the water (especially if it is mineral heavy)?

■ Will I have enough water and PSI (pounds per square inch) pressure to effectively run my Vichy system? On the average, each Vichy showerhead uses 2½ gallons of water per minute; there are now recirculating systems.

■ How high should I position my rainbar? How far apart should the showerheads be? How many showerheads do I need (four, five, or seven)? Ideally showerheads should be 18 inches apart. There is a 20° temperature loss between a ceiling mounted rainbar and one that extends from the wall (a higher mounting minimizes temperature loss).

Swiss showers (a water therapy treatment combining the use of stationary water jets aimed at pressure areas of the body; the water alternates between cold and warm to stimulate circulation and relieve tension) are basically stand-up Vichy systems. You may choose either a modular or a built-in-wall shower system. A client who chose to build one encountered problems with water pressure and showerhead placement. There are many manufacturers and distributors that have a variety of models.

Light Therapy Systems

Light therapy systems are designed similar to the rainbar of a Vichy shower, only instead of showerheads they have seven individual rays of color that will help balance the body's seven Chakras (more about this in Chapter 5). Light and color therapy is a very powerful healing system; however, individuals marketing the service and/or treatment need to believe in the value and benefits of it. Therapists need to have specialized training in the healing effects of color and Chakras.

There are many new era capsules for spa treatments. Using the new era capsules for spa treatments offers the additional benefit to spa revenue because the therapist does not need to be paid. Two options are explained here:

1. **Sunspatra 9000** provides conditioning and rehabilitation treatment for the whole body. Synergistic sensory stimulation strengthens, rejuvenates, and calms the mind and body for peak performance, harmony, and optimum chemical balance. The main features include:

   - Dry heat sauna
   - Vibratory massage
   - Back thigh heat pad
   - Stereo sound system
   - Ionized face air
   - Full-spectrum light
   - Chromatherapy/color light
   - Alpha/theta stimulus light
   - Aromatherapy

2. **Alpha 33** provides massage vibration, adjustable heat, and aromatherapy to enhance treatments such as the following:

- Weight loss/slimming and reduction
- Body wraps
- Exfoliation
- Massage
- Facials
- Detoxification
- Relaxation
- Moisturizing

Flotation tanks open a new market for meditation-centered clients. By minimizing sensory information, the brain can more easily become attuned to the alpha state of relaxation. You need to research your market for interest or believe in the philosophy and be able to market the service. Always consider the cost and number of treatments you would need to perform to recover your investment, and find out when you will see a return on that investment.

Oxygen therapy has become very popular. There are many systems and methods now being used, such as ozone sauna cabinets offering oxygenated steam therapy, specific machines for air oxygen therapy, oxygen bars, and specialized product lines.

Endermologie (massage therapy that reduces the appearance of cellulite while defining the figure) *and/or endermatic* massage systems offer specific lymphatic drainage, cellulite reduction, and slimming and reducing treatments.

Bioharmonic therapy generators are being used for noninvasive face lifts, lymphatic drainage, balancing Chakras, and many more technologically advanced treatments. Bioharmonic electric frequencies have been used successfully for decades to stimulate and balance the body's production of neurotransmitters and endorphins. New world trends give you the opportunity to use this advanced yet ancient technology.

If you are ready to embrace a state-of-the-art, cutting-edge technology doctors believe may enhance the potential of all life energy, one that is already becoming **nouveauté** (newness, novelty, change and innovation) in the spa industry, do your research. A good place to start is the Energy Enhancement System at <www.energyenhancementsystem.com>. This system, capable of emulating the energy transmitted in hands-on-healing, was designed by Sandra Rose Michael over a period of 12 years. Sandra Rose has been listed in the *Who's Who* and is a recognized Kahuna healer that has taught holistic health for nearly 30 years. The system generates fields. From their research, doctors believe these fields allow cellular regeneration and create right–left brain synchronization as demonstrated with electroencephalogram testing.

The Energy Enhancement System technology has been presented at more than a dozen national and international medical, scientific, and other conferences including the American Anti-Aging Medicine and the Radiation Oncology Committee Meeting. A number of spas across the country have embraced this technology.

By increasing your knowledge of what is available in the world of spa/salon equipment and supplies, you have more options when it comes to making decisions on what equipment and supplies you will choose to purchase for your facility. Keeping abreast of the latest in technology and the diversified marketplace allows you to offer your client the leading-edge equipment. Always keep in mind that consumers are knowledgeable, educated, and well traveled and demand the latest and the best.

Concepts for Consideration

1. What factors need to be considered before purchasing your stylists' chairs?
2. Of what relevance is identifying exactly how much water is required to operate a Vichy shower?
3. How would personally experiencing some spa/salon services and treatments in spas/salons be of value and benefit to you before you join the workforce, build your spa/salon, and or sell products and equipment to clients?
4. Why would identifying all the types/categories of equipment available in the spa/salon industry marketplace be of importance?
5. How would using an accelerator machine benefit your business operations?

5

Transforming Body, Mind, and Spirit

The body is a unified energy field: an integrated whole, where
body, mind, and spirit are one.

Our bodies are many worlds in one. Depending on our individual **perceptions** (a mindset we use to view the world and how we view ourselves; it is shaped by our experiences, education, and beliefs), the human form is wondrous, magical, and mysterious. Because we work on this wondrous body in the spa/salon industry, performing specific services and treatments on clients, it is incredibly important to understand some fundamental and newly emerging holistic world views, as well as the ancient wisdom of the body, mind, and spirit.

Thanks to research into the structure of matter and the behavior of energy, scientists now understand that the basic underlying reality behind all existence is not matter but **consciousness** (awareness, cognizance, and knowingness)—a common thread in ancient mystical teachings.

"The body cannot be cured without regard for the soul."

Socrates

According to the Divine Concept, we all exist within a field of consciousness of pure energy and light. It is at this subatomic level where the Divine Concept of Oneness sustains the life force within, otherwise known as ***prana*** or **chi** (life force energy). It is also here where higher consciousness is realized because mind energy and information are everything in the universe.

The universe consists of solids, liquids, and gases and is constantly in motion. Every existing thing is identified by its own vibration frequency, defined as the number of periodic **oscillations** (fluctuating and moving back and forth between two points), vibrations, or waves per unit of time. Because sound, light, and brain waves are measured mathematically, we know that each form and creation has a mathematic formula that comprises its essence. Resonating with Divine Oneness enables the individual mind to create and manifest. The key to accessing that power lies in an individual's ability to remain calm, balanced, and at peace during all situations.

This is an incredibly exciting time for individuals within the spa/salon industry. The possibilities for new treatments and services are extensive if you are creative, innovative, and open to new ideas. The purpose of spa/salons, through evolution, will be to create experiences that help individuals access the Divine Oneness through bodywork, health and beauty treatments, and alternative therapies. Most people today face their greatest challenge in integrating body, mind, and spirit.

Inner and Outer Beauty

A physicist defines the body as being composed of **atoms**—particles moving at lightning speed around huge empty spaces that emerge from a field of pure energy or potentiality. The emerging particles are fluctuations of energy and information. So, in reality, our personal essence of nonphysical energy radiates through our physical form, our body.

Dr. Deepak Chopra, a pioneer in futuristic medicine, has integrated the ancient wisdom of Eastern **Ayurvedic** medicine with Western science. Ayurvedic medicine is a type of medicine practiced in India for more than 5,000 years that identifies a person's constitution and treats the person with diet, exercise, meditation, herbs, massage, sun, and breathing to bring harmony to the physical, mental, and spiritual health of the individual. He also created a paradigm for exploring the healing process—a model called Quantum Healing, which examines the remedial practice from a more natural perspective by integrating body, mind, and spirit.

All the ancient and mystical teachings about body, mind, and spirit can be validated by our advanced technology. Medical research and advanced technology are ahead of the average person's comprehension of the nature of the immune system, the roles of the endocrine system, and cellular reprogramming. Most individuals are searching for information and services to increase vitality, youthfulness, longevity, beauty, and a sense of serenity. According to Chopra, healing cannot be comprehended unless the person's beliefs, assumptions, expectations, and self-image are also understood. In this context, workers in the spa/salon industry need to approach the well-being of their clients at more holistic, physical, mental, emotional, and spiritual levels.

How do people truly feel about themselves when they come in for a facial and want the fine lines refined? What about the client who is all bound up, with blocked energy and tight, cramping muscles? Dr. Maxwell Maltz, one of the world's most highly respected plastic surgeons, wrote some very insightful books before his death. He realized plastic surgery cannot only alter a person's face but the inner self as well. The incisions a surgeon makes are more than skin deep; they also frequently cut further into the psyche. Once he explored this area, he discovered that the "self-image," or the individual's mental and spiritual concept of self, was the key to personality and behavior. You must believe and trust in yourself and feel good about yourself, which in turn will create wholesome self-esteem and generate a positive self-image. If we feel good about how we look, we are happier and more empowered.

Better Living through Body Biochemistry

Our thoughts and feelings affect our body biochemistry. Our cells are constantly processing and metabolizing our experiences, based on our personal perceptions. As you internalize an event, you physically *tune in* to your interpretation. An individual's interpretation of aging is critical to what happens to them in the future. According to ayurveda, aging is merely the loss of cellular intelligence. A cell can avoid decay and remain new if it has the ability to preserve its complete store of intelligence. The unseen or nonphysical world is the real world, and if you are willing to explore this nonphysical level of your body, you will begin to understand its intelligence at a cellular level.

Endocrinology is the study of the endocrine system and its glands, which are chemical factories that create complex compounds called **hormones** (chemical substances formed in one organ or part of the body and carried in the blood to another organ or part which it stimulates to functional activity or secretion). These hormonal secretions exert specific regulatory effects on a wide variety of the body's normal chemical processes. The last 10 years of research have determined that when we have a thought, a feeling, or an emotion, our brains create a set of chemicals called neuropeptides, enabling brain cells to speak to each other. Cells in the immune system have receptors for these neuropeptides, so your immune cells are listening to your thoughts and self-talk. The immune system is like a circulating nervous system and can create the same chemicals you would find in brain cells. When you have a gut feeling, your receptors are actually responding to these chemicals.

According to Chopra, we have about 60,000 thoughts a day—95 percent of those thoughts you have today are the same ones you had yesterday, so we create the same patterns that give rise to the same physical expressions of the body. Experiments show that risk factors for heart disease are smoking, hypertension, and being overweight. More than 50 percent of people who have heart attacks do not have the risk factors. The result of the study validated the two most important factors for heart disease: job satisfaction and self-happiness.

More people die Monday morning at 9 a.m. than at any other time of the week. They would rather die than go to work where they are not fulfilled.

Through an understanding of how our nonphysical or energetic system affects the physical body's organization structure, you will begin to realize the cellular intelligence of the body. Integrating both the nonphysical and physical anatomic aspects of the body will assist individuals in the spa/salon industry in understanding and implementing the advanced technologies and the holistic emerging world views into their spa/salon services and treatments.

The Physical Body's Organization Structure

The processes of diseases and their causes are as follows:

- Destructive emotions and thoughts (fear, anger, stress, resentment), which affect the internal organs and the immune system
- Toxic accumulation within the body resulting from poor circulation, poor elimination, and lack of exercise
- Improper posture and body structure, including misaligned spines, blood and lymph stagnation, and poor muscle tone
- Unhealthy diets, excessive alcohol, coffee, drugs, and tobacco

The Physical Body's Organization Structure		*Table 5–1*
Chemical level	Includes atoms and molecules essential for maintaining life	
Cellular level	Includes molecules from cells, which are the basic structural and functional units of an organism	
Tissue level	Includes tissues, which are groups of similar cells (and the surrounding substance) that perform a specific function	
Organ level	Includes structures that are composed of two or more different tissues, having specific functions and recognizable shapes	
System level	Includes several related organisms that have a common function	
Organismic level	Includes all parts of the body functioning together that comprises the total organism—a living being	

Our Body Systems

An understanding of our body's systems and vital functions will help you become more proficient at performing professional spa and salon services.

Skeletal System

- Provides physical form for the body
- Consists of ligaments; fibrous tissue that holds the bones together at the joints and connects organs to one another; and cartilage, which covers the ends of the bones at the joints

Muscular System

- Gives shape, support, and substance to the skeletal system
- Comprises 40 percent to 50 percent of the body weight
- Muscles and bones are joined by tendons, forming the musculoskeletal system
- Muscles and nerves form the neuromuscular system

To Chinese physicians, the body is a series of energy conduits with a mysterious life force known as Chi flowing along systematic meridians with pressure points. By inserting needles into specific points on the body, and/or massaging pressure points, they can restore the unseen Chi that is out of balance or blocked. In Chinese medicine, the liver controls the muscles and muscle activity, while the spleen sends Chi to the muscles and is responsible for muscle tone.

Functions of the liver include the following:

- Produces bile and contributes to healthy digestion
- Detoxifies the blood
- Provides blood and Chi to the muscles, tendons, ligaments, and eyes
- Influences the ability to sleep deeply
- Controls stomach and spleen
- Maintains emotions, especially anger

According to the principles of acupuncture, the liver meridian originates at the rib cage, directly above the liver on the right side, and over the spleen on the left side. It travels downward along the groin area and inside of the leg, over the inner part of the knee, down the calf, over the ankle and foot, to the big toe of each foot. If the liver is congested or unhealthy, the Chi will not flow smoothly through the organ and will be unsettled, active, and even chaotic. This results in a sense of internal conflict and excessive thinking, which sometimes causes insomnia.

Nervous System

- The nervous system is the most advanced communication system on earth—coordinating, integrating, and controlling all the other systems to create harmony.
- Every square inch of the body is supplied with nerves.
- The nervous and endocrine systems are so interdependent, they are sometimes referred to as the neurohumoral system.
- The nervous system operates largely through electrical and chemical mechanisms.
- The endocrine system functions through chemical hormones.
- The brain, spinal column, and their nerves are the principal parts of the nervous system.

The brain is the place where visible meets invisible and where flesh and blood mingle with thoughts, instinct, emotion, and spirit. There are four kinds of brain waves indicating electrical activity, which can be recorded by an electroencephalogram.

Alpha Waves

■ Present when normal individuals are awake in a resting state with their eyes closed; these waves disappear during sleep

■ Rhythmic waves occurring at the rate of about 8 to 13 cycles per second (Hertz)

■ Hertz (Hz) expresses the frequency; 1 Hz = 1 cycle per second

Beta Waves

■ Present when the nervous system is active; when there is sensory input and mental activity

■ Rhythmic waves with a frequency between 14 and 30 Hz

Delta Waves

■ Present during deep sleep

■ Rhythmic waves with a frequency of 1 to 5 Hz

Theta Waves

■ Dominant in children ages 2 to 5 years

■ Waves with a frequency of 4 to 7 Hz

We look around and wonder why so many individuals are living chaotic, unhappy lives. Emotional stress creates chemical imbalances, which do not allow calmness or clarity for individuals when they make certain decisions and behave in particular ways. Rather than using chemicals, drugs, and alcohol, individuals can learn meditation or experience specific spa therapies and treatments to calm and balance themselves.

Approximately 50 substances, known as neurotransmitters, exist in the brain and transmit nerve impulses across the gap between the neurons. Several of these neurotransmitters are known to be hormones, which are released into the body by the endocrine cells in organs throughout the body. **Enkephalin** (an endorphin having opiate qualities that occurs in the brain, spinal cord, and elsewhere) and other **endorphins** (neurochemicals occurring naturally in the brain) have potent analgesic (pain-relieving) effects. The analgesic effects of acupuncture may be the result of increased releases of enkephalin or endorphins. The incredible, pleasurable sensation felt after making love results from the release of *endorphins*.

If you are interpreting an event as stressful, the body makes *jittery molecules* and toxins, or free-radical compounds. It is the way we interpret reality that generates the molecules our bodies make.

The brain makes the following:

- Acetylcholine

Low levels cause the following:

Forgetfulness

Inability to concentrate

Sleeplessness

Poor muscle coordination

- Norepinephrine

Low levels cause the following:

Depression

- Serotonin

Low levels of **serotonin** (a neurotransmitter in the brain) cause the following:

Sleep disorders

Smell, the most sensitive of our senses, is directly linked with the limbic system. Scents and fragrances stimulate an array of emotional, psychological, and physical responses among individuals. That is why it is so important to have a good working knowledge of aromatherapy in spa/salon facilities wanting to integrate this practice into their lines of services and treatments.

The *spinal cord*, located within the vertebral canal of the vertebral column, originates in the brain, extends the length of the trunk, and is protected by the spinal column, which encloses it. A spinal nerve network called the plexus (braid) is formed on both sides of the body.

The principal plexuses are as follows:

- Cervical plexus
- Brachial plexus
- Lumbar plexus
- Sacral plexus

The sympathetic nervous system consists of a double chain of small ganglia (masses of neurons) extending along the spinal column from the base of the brain to the coccyx. This information is very relevant because it also becomes an intricate part of understanding the nonphysical body or *spirit anatomy.*

Circulatory System

- The circulatory system consists of the heart and the blood vessels.
- Red blood cells carry oxygen to the cells.
- White blood cells destroy disease-causing germs.
- Plasma is the fluid part of the blood in which the red and white blood cells and platelets flow.

Blood plasma is nine-tenths water and is almost identical to seawater, both in composition and concentration of mineral salts, proteins, and trace elements. Algae possess the same mineral salts and trace elements with added vitamins but in higher concentration than seawater. Any body treatments with algae are extremely beneficial to the body. Plasma carries food, nutrients, and secretions to the cells and carbon dioxide from the cells.

The *lymph-vascular system* consists of lymph, a colorless, watery liquid derived from the blood plasma, trading nutritive materials to the cells in return for waste products of metabolism. This fluid is absorbed into the lymph capillaries; it is filtered and detoxified as it passes through the lymph nodes and is eventually reintroduced into the bloodstream. Most of us have experienced being ill with swollen lymph glands at one time in our lives.

Endocrine System

- The endocrine system is composed of organs (glands) that produce hormones that are transported through the blood and lymph.
- Major function of the endocrine system is to assist the nervous system in regulating body processes.
- Every organ that produces hormones can be considered an endocrine gland.

According to the Chinese, when these organs are balanced, the mind is balanced—emotional and psychological harmony is the result. Endocrine glands are continuously responding to the current conditions within the bloodstream, as well as glandular functions.

Pituitary Gland (Master Gland)
- Located at the base of the brain, within the brainstem
- Regulates the activities of all the other endocrine glands

Pineal Gland (Third Eye)

- Located in the brainstem.
- Maintains biorhythms, brain chemistry, and moods

Thyroid Gland

- Located at the base of the neck toward the front
- Regulates metabolism, respiration, and oxygen consumption by the cells

Thymus Gland

- The thymus gland is located in the upper part of the chest just below the breastbone.
- Chronic stress shrinks the thymus gland and impairs its function.
- A healthy thymus gland is essential to a healthy immune system.
- Positive emotions and an optimistic attitude toward life enhance the functioning of the thymus.

Pancreas

- Located in the center of the abdomen
- Secretes digestive juices that assist in digestion and production of the hormone insulin that uses blood sugars as fuel

Adrenal Glands (Suprarenal)—Stress Glands

- Located at the top of each kidney and are highly susceptible to stress

Reproductive Glands

- The testes produce testosterone, the hormone that controls sex characteristics in males.
- The ovaries produce estrogen and progesterone that are essential to the development of female characteristics.
- *Leydig* cells within the testes and ovaries produce testosterone, which is associated with libido and sexual energy in both males and females.

Integumentary System—The Skin

- The skin is the largest organ of the body, performing many vital functions required for health, well-being, and beauty.
- The skin is rich with all the same hormones that are in the brain.

- Stimulation of the skin causes a shower of healing chemicals into the bloodstream.

- The **epidermis,** or outer layer of the skin, is made of soft keratin. The keratinization process, which takes roughly 27 days, involves a cell formed in the basal layer rising to the surface of the epidermal layer, where it becomes keratinized and sloughed off.

- The **dermis,** the middle layer of the skin, is composed of connective tissue containing collagen and elastin fibers. Elastin is a protein that fills the spaces between the collagen fibers, giving the skin its elasticity. A breakdown in this connective tissue causes wrinkles.

The skin is nourished by the blood and lymph system. Anywhere between one-half to one-third of the total blood supply of the body is distributed to the skin. This is why facial and body treatments and massage are so effective. The skin has sensory receptors connected to the spinal cord by nerve fibers called tactile points. Tactile signals from the skin pass via spinal cord into the somesthetic area of the brain, responsible for creating electrical and chemical changes.

Associations between the brain and the skin are extremely intimate, as shown in a lie detector test. In the test, specific mental states directly influence the electrical properties of the skin and can be measured and correlated. Skin sensitivity is so great that when combined with its ability to pick up and transmit an incredible variety of signals, it can also make a wide variety of responses. Our skin reacts to someone's touch in different ways. Considering all the vital functions of the skin and its ability to absorb cosmetics, chemicals, and drugs, we understand why knowledge of these properties is of prime importance in the spa/salon industry. Touch, music, color, scent, and speech all change the neuropeptides in the brain.

The Chakra System

Chakra is a Sanskrit word meaning wheel or disk and refers to seven basic energy centers within what is called the subtle or **etheric** (celestial or heavenly; the regions of space) body. The **aura,** the external manifestation of the subtle body, is made up of the more spiritual aspects of ourselves, experienced as thoughts, feelings, and emotions. Chakras are not to be thought of as synonymous with any portion of the physical body; they are superimposed on the physical body as an electromagnetic field. "The Chakra is our *spiritual anatomy,*" says Dr. Caroline Myss, author of the book, *Anatomy of the Spirit,* and a pioneer in energy medicine and human consciousness.

In 1937 Dr. Semyon Kirilian attracted scientific attention when he created halo effects on film. This process, now known as *Kirilian* (also known as *Kirlian*) photography, led the Russian scientist to believe that the halo images represented life energy, the aura.

Someone who has spent nearly 20 years researching Kirilian photography is Dr. Agnnes Kraweck, a graduate from Donsbach University School of Nutrition in California and a world-renowned lecturer and media personality. Many of her findings have surfaced in books such as *Kirilian Aura Photography* and *Life's Hidden Forces, A Personal Journey into Kirilian Photography,* both available in 41 countries around the globe.

"We have reached a stage in our evolution where focus and attention will be on *health, longevity, relaxation, and the transformation of human consciousness,*" says Agnnes. "Good health is the foundation of physical, mental, emotional, and spiritual well-being. Living past 100 years in a healthy, vibrant body will become a natural occurrence as we discover our own power to heal in health and the healing process."

Agnnes believes a new and more holistic approach to health is quickly emerging with the awareness that not only does the Spirit have a physical experience, but that we can find all the answers to our questions by looking within. In her practice, Agnnes uses *Kirilian* photography to follow energy movement through different electromagnetic highways in the physical body and record that energy flow in mental, physical, emotional, and intuitive fields. She also uses an intuitive tool called an "aura meter," which demonstrates how the physical body responds to these fields. From these readings, Agnnes can find out if a person's energy is nutritionally balanced, discover intuitive or psychic abilities, detect longstanding unresolved issues, or ascertain whether someone has healing capacity. "Anytime a therapy is given that involves the hands, a healing may take place, especially if there is a vibrational match between a giver and a receiver," says Agnnes. Agnnes believes human consciousness is evolving faster globally in both young and old.

The Chakras resemble funnel-shaped blossoms, each possessing a different number of petals, which is why they are often referred to as lotus blossoms in the East. The petals of the blossoms represent **nadis** (energy channels within the subtle bodies), which take in and process energy of a higher vibrational nature so that it may be properly assimilated and used to transform the physical body. From the deepest point at the center of each Chakra, a stemlike channel extends to the spine and merges with the *Sushumna,* the most important energy channel.

Eastern metaphysics talks about three channels of energy that flow through the body along the spine: the *Ida,* the *Pingala,* and the *Sushumna* (the moon, the sun, and the balance of the two). The Sushumna acts as a super highway for these energies. Traveling beside, around, and through this highway are many acupuncture meridians and thousands of nadis. Two basic currents of energy run through the body and connect all the Chakras: the liberating current (cosmic or divine consciousness) and the manifesting current (*Kundalini*). The intersection of the two currents creates the Chakras.

The Chakras are aspects of consciousness that interact with the physical body through two major vehicles: the endocrine system and the nervous system. The seven Chakras are associated with the endocrine glands; a particular group of nerves called a *plexus;* and nerve ganglia, where there is a high degree of nervous activity (Fig. 5–1).

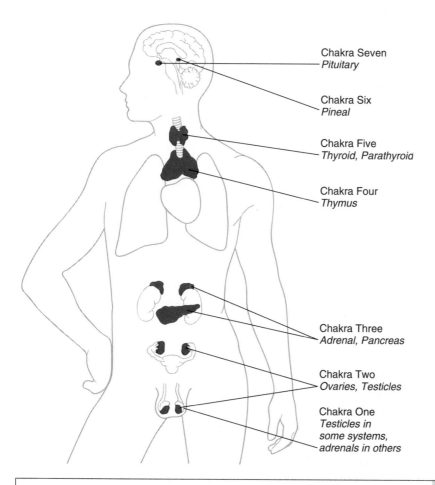

Chakra Seven
Pituitary

Chakra Six
Pineal

Chakra Five
Thyroid, Parathyroid

Chakra Four
Thymus

Chakra Three
Adrenal, Pancreas

Chakra Two
Ovaries, Testicles

Chakra One
Testicles in
some systems,
adrenals in others

Common associations between the Chakras and the glands of the endocrine system. Some systems reverse Chakras 6 and 7, making pineal a seventh Chakra gland and making the pituitary related to the sixth.

Figure 5–1

"The endocrine glands are a part of the powerful master control system that affects the physiology of the body from the level of cellular gene activation on up to the functioning of the central nervous system," says Dr. Richard Gerber, in the *Third Edition of Vibrational Medicine.*

"The Chakras, which process vibrational energy of specific frequencies are thus able to affect our moods and behavior through hormonal influences on brain activity. Recent scientific research in the field of **psychoneuroimmology** (a specialized field of research that studies the relationship between the brain and the immune system, and how they communicate with each other using various chemical messengers) has begun to hint at deeper connections between the brain, endocrine, and immune systems than had been previously recognized. The Chakras play a vital role in the regulation of various states of consciousness, especially in regard to peoples' emotional nature. Although the digestive system takes in biochemical energy and molecular building blocks in the form of physical nutrients, the Chakras, in conjunction with the acupuncture meridian system, take in vibrational energies that are just as integral to the proper growth and maintenance of physical life. Whereas the physical nutrients are used to promote cellular growth and homeostasis at the molecular level, the subtle energy currents conveyed by the Chakras and meridians assist in promoting stability and organization within the etheric body, which is the growth template for the physical. Energetic changes occur at the etheric level before becoming manifest as physical cellular events."

The physical body is the end result of a process that begins with consciousness. The direction of manifestation flows as shown in the margin to the left:

Consciousness

Energy   Field

Physical   Body

We have an inner guidance system that speaks a simple language—either it feels good or it doesn't. Your consciousness is who you are—your experience of being. Your structure perceives, analyzes, stores, retrieves, and creates information about any subject whatsoever, whether it be internal, external, real, or imagined. When you feel tension in your consciousness, you feel it on a physical level in your body associated with that Chakra. When the tension continues over a period of time, or reaches a critical intensity, you create a physical symptom. The symptom lets you know about what you are doing to yourself in your consciousness. It is interesting that the tension shows up in the energy field before there is any evidence of it at the physical level.

In metaphysical terminology, a Chakra is a vortex of energy made up of our own mental and physical programming. These templates remain lodged in the Chakras as part of our consciousness, governing our actions. The way we *feel* dictates our *actions.* This in turn determines the type of experiences we are likely to have, governing the energy that the Chakra is likely to draw to itself. The shape and content of the Chakras are formed largely by repeated patterns from our actions. In day-to-day life, because we are always the center point of these actions, repeated movements and habits create forms and actions in the world around us.

According to some theories, programming from parents and culture, physical body shape, situations we are born into, and information from previous lives are also important factors. Interpretations of these actions can provide guidelines to the tendencies of the person but denote nothing is unchangeable. It is common to become trapped in the self-perpetuating actions of any one Chakra. The object is to release, eliminate, and clear the Chakras of old, nonbeneficial patterns to create actions that have a positive influence on our life journey. A block in one Chakra can affect the others, similar to a misaligned vertebra affecting the whole spine.

Chakras are centers for receiving, assimilating, and transmitting life energies. The seven Chakras vibrate at a certain frequency in a logical and sequential order, just like colors of the spectrum and notes on a musical scale. In fact, colors and musical notes correspond to Chakras. Music played in a certain key vibrates with a particular Chakra, and our feelings to the sounds depend on what type of music is playing. Natural essences and crystals have their own vibrations, which are specifically attuned to particular Chakras.

We can analyze the Chakras separately, always remembering they are interdependent facets of a basic unified field of consciousness. Where are we investing our energy (past, present, future, fear or love), and what part of our biology is paying the price? Through meditating; being in the moment; being mindful; and staying calm, centered, peaceful, and balanced during all situations, we automatically become dynamic, creative, and confident. We also become humble, loving, and compassionate. The process starts to develop when the kundalini rises and nourishes the Chakras.

"Too pragmatic and scientific to accept things on faith, Western peoples have lost touch with the world of spirit and the sense of unity it can bring. Ancient systems, couched in language and culture so different from ours, are often alienating for the Western mind," according to Anodea Judith, PhD and author of the book *Wheels of Life*. Ancient people created a profound system that can be integrated with modern technology and information about the natural world, the body, and the psyche to expand our understanding of body, mind, and spirit (Fig. 5–2).

Through modern physiology we see that the seven Chakras are located near the seven major nerve ganglia that emanate from the spinal column. The vertebrae are related to the different Chakras based on the spinal nerves and the ganglia and the glands of the endocrine system. In theory,

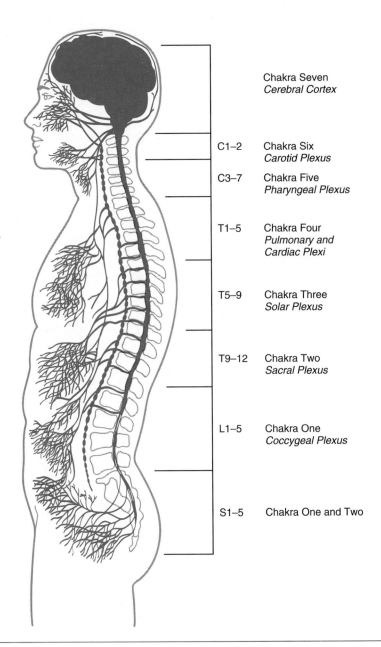

Chakra Seven
Cerebral Cortex

C1–2 Chakra Six
Carotid Plexus

C3–7 Chakra Five
Pharyngeal Plexus

T1–5 Chakra Four
*Pulmonary and
Cardiac Plexi*

T5–9 Chakra Three
Solar Plexus

T9–12 Chakra Two
Sacral Plexus

L1–5 Chakra One
Coccygeal Plexus

S1–5 Chakra One and Two

Figure 5–2	Shows the vertebrae related to the different Chakras based on the spinal nerves with the ganglia and various organs. If these vertebrae are damaged in a way that affects the spinal nerves, the related Chakras subsequently may be affected.

matter rules the lower Chakras, energy rules the middle Chakras, and consciousness rules the upper Chakras. Through understanding the Chakra system we can develop treatments and services in the spa/salon, which will integrate this knowledge, harmonizing, integrating, and balancing body, mind, and spirit.

Understanding the Chakras

Energy, consciousness, and matter intertwine to form all that we experience. Our body is an expression of ourselves.

Chakra #1

The first Chakra is called the "Root" (Fig. 5–3). Its Sanskrit name is Muldhara (root/support). It has the following qualities:

- Superimposed at the base of the spine below the sacrum bone between the anus and the genitals, connecting to the coccyx, the sacral plexus, and the coccygeal spinal ganglion
- Where the kundalini resides
- Associated with the following:
  Feet

  Legs

  Hips

  Sciatica

  Spinal column

  Bones

  Teeth/nails

  Blood

  Prostate gland

  Cell building

  Reproductive system

  Cells of leydig
- Associated with adrenal glands; hormones—adrenalin and nor-adrenaline
- Associated with the earth and understanding of the physical dimension. Therefore, it is our foundation, our sense of grounding

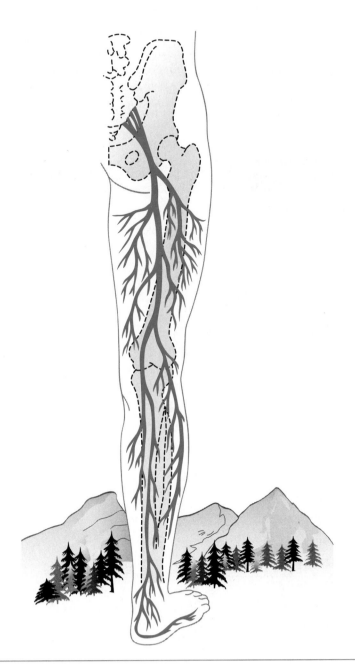

Figure 5–3   Chakra #1, sciatica nerve as a root.

in the physical plane. It is nothing but simplicity, purity, joy, and inner wisdom, which get clouded by our lifestyles.

- Balanced energy: gives us a sense of dignity, equilibrium, and a tremendous sense of direction and purpose in life

- Unbalanced energy: results in fear, lack of discipline, inability to achieve goals

- Color: red

- Musical note: C

- Gemstone: ruby, red garnet, red coral, bloodstone

- Element: sense, earth

- Essence: clove, cedar

- Verb: I have

Within your roots you find your past, your memories, your primal self (race, culture, heritage). Memories are lodged in the body of either pain or pleasure. This Chakra relates to all solid earthly things, such as our body, health, survival, material and monetary existence, and ability to focus and manifest our needs. The sciatic nerve, which travels down through the leg, functions like a root for our nervous system. If this Chakra is unbalanced, we lack a foundation, are ungrounded, and lack stability for longevity.

Through a process of *grounding*, we become solidly real, *present in the "now" moment,* dynamically alive with vitality—feeling ourselves as an integrated flow of energy. Without grounding we are unstable, tend to daydream, get swept off our feet, lose our center, become manipulated, and lose our ability to have or hold onto. When grounded, we have a feeling of stillness, solidity, and clarity, which brings relief from everyday life stresses. We live in a state of grace and are more detached, trusting, and objective about everything. That which has ground, substance, and validity finds its way to manifestation because each repeated thought and action condenses our ideas into solid form.

Few people are naturally grounded. Our cultural values reflect the superiority of our monetary, social, intellectual, and verbal skills over our physical, practical skills. We are taught to suppress our emotions. Natural body processes such as toileting, sexuality, birth, breastfeeding, or nudity are considered to be somewhat unacceptable or dirty—only to be done in private and sometimes with guilt. As we became more mechanized and urbanized, we lost touch with our earth; our health and our sense of self-worth have become more fragile. The stress of competition, fast living, and working daily does not give us a chance to process, release, and learn to let go. In an alienated and ungrounded world where most values do not favor the body or its pleasures, we deny our body feelings, whether they are pleasure or pain. If we feel pain, we become resistant to grounding because *to be grounded is to be in touch.*

"Since everything in the universe is energy and each individual has a different frequency, the common denominator for everyone is to ground their individual energy," says Vernon Wai, an electrical engineer who lives on the Big Island of Hawaii with his wife Swan. When I met Vern in 2002 I was very impressed with his intuition, grounded personality, and extraordinary skill in identifying gifted abilities in others.

"Grounding is about embracing oneself, providing oneself with completeness and living in harmony with oneself. Once you are grounded with clarity, you are still enough to understand the messages from the Divine. Being grounded is about being aware. When grounded, you know your gift and honor your specialty. I work with individuals to help them ground themselves and clarify their gifts. When two grounded individuals embrace each other in intimate or business relationships, magic is created. Find the gifts each other has to offer and live in harmony and joy with aloha Spirit," according to Vern.

The body can become overloaded and overstimulated by constant energies, which cause our internal systems to lose their delicate balance. Individuals facing that imbalance dull their senses with overworking, drugs, alcohol, food, shopping, sex, and other distractions instead of eliminating the stress and replacing it with natural vitality.

A grounded person has a dynamic clarity—a presence in the eyes and the body. The task of mastering the first Chakra is learning to accept our body, validate it, love it, and honor our feelings. The cosmic creative energies from the root Chakra can be used for creative expression or making babies. Developing our ability to create and *have* things begins with increasing self-worth. *To be here, in the moment,* we need to assert ourselves, claim our place, and secure our survival.

The purpose of the spa/salon is to help individuals feel good; look good; and increase well-being, self-worth, and beauty. Giving the body pleasurable remedies like massages, facials, and hydrotherapy—all tactile, sensuous experiences—can fulfill this purpose.

We also need to consider the mindset of spa/salon employees. Do they keep themselves grounded when working with so many people of different frequencies? How, in fact, do these caring, nurturing beings take care of themselves? What personal care and personal development systems do spa/salons have in place?

Chakra #2

The second Chakra is "Sacral" (Fig. 5–4). Its Sanskrit name is Svadhisthana (sweetness). It has the following qualities:

- Superimposed just below the navel, connected with the sacral and lumbar plexus
- Associated with the following:

  Lower back

  Hips

  Abdomen

  Pelvic area

  Reproductive system

- Associated with hormones—estrogen, testosterone
- Associated with water; giving us fluidity and grace, depth of feelings, sexual fulfillment, and the ability to accept change
- Associated with the understanding to honor one another and the willingness to feel their emotions
- Balanced energy: allows emotional and sensual expression
- Unbalanced energy: thinking too much drains energy, inability to feel emotions, fearful, overindulgent, impotent, or frigid
- Color: orange
- Music note: D
- Gemstone: moonstone, carnelian, coral
- Element: sense, water
- Essence: gardenia, ylang ylang, sandalwood
- Verb: I feel

This Chakra corresponds to the sacral vertebrae and the nerve ganglion called the sacral plexus. The plexus also hooks into the sciatic nerve and is the center of motion for the body. Desire is the expression of the physical, emotional, and spiritual needs of being, such as nourishment, warmth, touch, contact, and pleasure. The seed of our passion, joy, vitality, and power is desire. Pleasure is one of the essential features of the second Chakra and is essential for the health and harmony of the body, the rejuvenation of the spirit, and the healing of our personal and cultural relationships. In our society, we are taught to beware of pleasure. It is a dangerous temptress waiting to lure us from our true path. Through pleasures we learn to relax and release tension, soothing the nervous system.

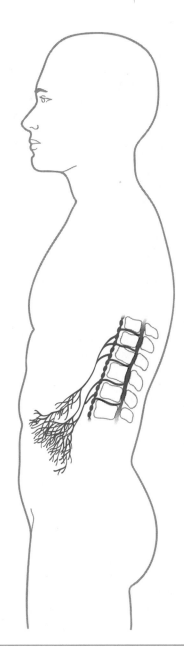

Figure 5-4   Chakra #2, sacral plexus and nerve ganglion.

Ignoring sensation levels of the body cuts us off from valuable feelings and emotions that play a part in transferring this information to the brain. Sensations are building blocks of our feelings and emotions. Without them we are lifeless forms and disconnected. There is a subtle difference between emotions and feelings. Feelings come before emotions; they are less formed and less tangible. Often we suppress our feelings precisely because they contain so little information. The expression of emotions is considered pleasurable—the suppression results in tension and pain. The absence of tension in the body creates an ease of movement similar to the grace and flow in animals. The suppression of pleasure creates a need for overindulgence, turning pleasure into pain. Pain is an indication we are going in the wrong direction.

Sexuality is a sacred ritual of union through the celebration of differences—an expansive movement of the life force, the dance that balances, restores, renews, and reproduces. It is a life force, although we live in a culture where it is either exploited or repressed. Denying the body intimacy and sexual release is nullifying access to some of the greatest pleasure the body can have. This denial also cuts us off from the subtle feelings and emotions housed in the lower Chakras. Passage of energy between a couple engaged in sexual activity is far more than a physical union. Chakras are aligned between the partners. Each Chakra vibrates more intensely, and the passage of energy from one body to another is enhanced and woven on all levels, if the partners' frequencies are similar. Couples can mutually choose to focus energy on a physical, mental, or emotional level.

Clairessence is the psychic sense of the second Chakra, the first stirring of *higher consciousness* and the development of greater sensitivity to others. You gain the ability to sense other people's emotions through empathy.

Spas and salons can create nurturing, sensual experiences for their clients to fulfill these desires. Hydrotherapies, with the fluidity of the water in specific body treatments, and many other creative ideas could help individuals seeking pleasure. With so many people missing out on pleasurable experiences, we need to look at specific services and treatments to help them feel better.

Chakra #3

The third Chakra is called "Solar Plexus" (Fig. 5–5). Its Sanskrit name is Manipura (lustrous jewel). It has the following qualities:

- Superimposed on the solar plexus between the navel and the chest, connected with lumbar vertebrae

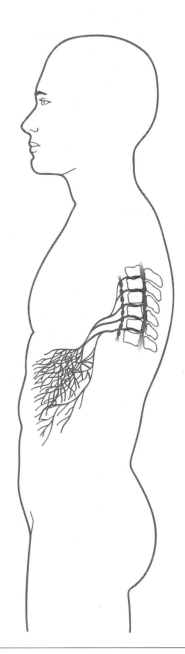

Figure 5–5   Chakra #3, solar plexus, navel Chakra.

- Associated with the following:

  Pancreas

  Liver

  Stomach

  The skin as a system

  Face

  Adrenal glands

  Gall bladder

  Digestive system

  Autonomic nervous system

  Muscular system

- Associated with the hormone insulin

- Associated with fire, giving us a sense of generosity, satisfaction, and contentment

- Balanced energy: gives us integrity and endurance, associated with our respect and belief in self

- Known as the power Chakra; ruling our personal power, will, and metabolism

- When enlightened by the kundalini, we have an inner sense of morality and balance at all levels

- Unbalanced energy: fearful, scattered, constantly active, angry, confused, difficulty breathing, liver problems, diabetes, pancreas and gall bladder problems

- Color: yellow

- Music note: E

- Gemstone: topaz, amber, tiger's eye, citrine

- Element: sense, fire/sight

- Essence: rosemary, bergamot, lavender

- Verb: I can

Rather than defining **power** as control over something, we need to understand the concept of power as integration from within. Power uses intelligence to coordinate interactions in the world; synthesizing ideas from the mind prepares them for manifestation. To have power, we need to be conscious, understand relationships between things, perceive and assimilate new information, and create and imagine events outside of present time and space. Power, which is applied knowledge, must be developed

WAYS TO CLAIM YOUR POWER

- Do something different; if active, be still and do not cling to security.

- Take care of yourself, know what you want and give it to yourself.

- Avoid invalidation, and do not take criticism from others who do not understand your situation; a truly sensitive person takes it to heart.

- Break attachment if the energy toward something is not manifesting results. Let it go.

- Pay attention: notice where you focus your energy, whether it be the past, the present, or the future. Know who or what you focus your energy on, paying attention to what you need.

- Become grounded. Direct your attention to the *here and now* to manifest your power. Grounding brings us into the present moment; mindfulness consolidates and focuses that energy.

- Acknowledge your anger and let it go. Blocked power is often blocked anger.

- Increase your information, learn more, and apply your knowledge.

- Love. It increases our strength and inspires.

consciously. Powerlessness is the result of ignorance, lack of awareness, or lack of detail.

Technology and knowledge are ways of harnessing existing power. Create services and treatments in the spa/salon with conscious awareness and knowledge of what individuals need and desire. Take advantage of new information and technology.

Chakra #4

The fourth Chakra is the "Heart Center" (Fig. 5–6). Its Sanskrit name is Anahata (unstruck). It has the following qualities:

- Superimposed at the heart center, between the should blades and the sternum
- Associated with the following:

  Thymus gland

  Heart

  Lungs

  Immune system

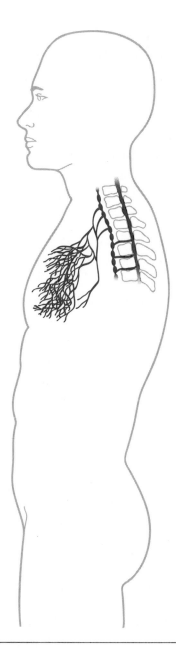

Chakra #4, the heart Chakra.

Figure 5-6

Blood circulatory system

Connected to the cardiac plexus

- Related to love, self-acceptance, compassion, peace, harmony, balance, and beauty

- Purpose, to achieve perfect union through love

- Unbalanced energy: demanding, moody, shy, lonely, critical, codependent, feelings of unworthiness, difficulty in breathing

- Connector of the three lower physical Chakras with the three higher mental and spiritual Chakras

- Color: green/pink

- Musical note: F

- Gemstone: emerald, green jade, rose quartz, pink tourmaline

- Element: sense, air/touch

- Essence: lavender, jasmine, marjoram, rose

- Verb: I love

From the world of body and manifestation, we move into the softer touch of spirit. Integration and balancing the realms of the body and mind bring a sense of peace and wholeness. It is here that our deep wishes of the soul are felt. Our dreams, hopes, wishes, and fears are deeper and more integral to our own sense of being than the second Chakra. Love, at this heart level, is felt within us as a state of being, not of object dependency or need. A joyous acceptance of our place among all things and a deep sense of peace come from the lack of need—a sense of harmony, balance, and peace within the self. At the second Chakra, more sexual, passionate love flourishes. Very object-oriented passion is stimulated and dictated by the presence of a person, place, or thing; a feeling of emptiness results when these things are absent. Second Chakra love is a more transitory passion, where love in the heart is more enduring, eternal, and constant. Fourth-level Chakra love reaches out to others with a radiating quality and never leaves its own center. In relationships there is no fighting—only harmony, acceptance, free flowing lightness, simplicity, softness, calm, and evenness.

Opening the heart Chakra requires a combination of technique and understanding. You learn to see the world in terms of relationships with their balance and affinity. The subatomic world is one of rhythms, movement, and continual change. Movement, matter, and perpetual interactions unite definite, nonrandom sets of relationships. These relationships are the key to ongoing cycles, fixed by a certain cosmic order and built by observable laws and forces. Balance within ourselves allows us to perceive and enter into the equilibrium of all lasting patterns of relationships. When we consciously temper our will and fulfill our needs, our minds can better enter into this understanding of relationships and we can find our proper place. From this place, all our relationships, as well as their beginnings and endings, are in harmony with a greater pattern. The relationships with the greatest equilibrium, and therefore the most grace, will necessarily be the most permanent, whereas transitory relationships are stepping stones in the swirling creation of a larger pattern. For the purpose of growth, understand that we are always in our proper place. The realization of the heart Chakra is a joyous acceptance of the perfection of this place and *this opens the heart to receive.*

Imbalances within the heart Chakra throw the entire system off balance between the upper and lower Chakras, resulting in imbalances between mind and body, inner and outer, self and transcendence. By living in balance, within a state of grace, delicacy, and gentleness, we achieve harmony with oneself. Energy we project outwards finds a matching energy that reaches us. If we emanate a loving, accepting, and joyful vibration, we encourage another's own sense of affinity.

Self-love is the important underlying balance that supports any long-term relationship. When our heart Chakra is open and balanced, our very presence radiates joy and love. Love is the pure essence of healing. On a societal level, we are dealing with more heart issues in the medical community. Spa and salon employees can help individuals enjoy nurturing experiences by doing their own self-healing—so they can radiate the joy and love to all.

Chakra #5

The fifth Chakra is the "Throat" Chakra (Fig. 5–7). Its Sanskrit name is Visshudha (purification). Its qualities are as follows:

- Superimposed at the throat area and connected to the pharyngeal plexus thyroid
- Associated with the following:

  Parathyroids

  Neck

  Arms

  Hands

  Jaw

  Vocal cords

  Mouth

  Teeth
- Associated with the hormone **thyroxine** (natural hormone produced by the thyroid gland)

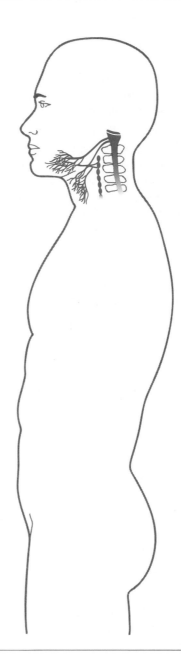

| *Figure 5–7* | Chakra #5. |

- Associated with self-expression, clear communication, creativity, compassion, and discernment

- Balanced energy: gives the ability to express one's thoughts and feelings; allows you to receive, gives the ability to listen to your intuition and to see your goals manifest—a state of *grace* and *abundance*

- Unbalanced energy: excessive talking, inability to listen, lack of discernment, thyroid and immune problems, fear, inability to express thoughts and feelings

- Color: blue/silver

- Musical note: G

- Gemstone: blue sapphire, turquoise, aquamarine

- Element: sense, ether/sound

- Essence: frankincense, sage, eucalyptus

- Verb: I speak

Communication is the connecting principle that makes life possible. The fifth Chakra is the realm of consciousness that controls, creates, transmits, and receives communication both *within the self and with each other.* Heart connections are made with others, and the tone of voice is more important than the words. Awareness of the world at a vibration level becomes greater. We need to be aware of what *messages* our body is giving us and acknowledge, listen, and honor what it needs. Otherwise, how can we do that for others or expect that of others? We affect each other with vibrations we carry within our minds and bodies. If we understand communication to be the art of transmitting and receiving information, we need to learn to balance our Chakra energies and calm our minds and thoughts so that our consciousness becomes as smooth as a soft wind or calm ocean.

Sound, rhythm, and vibration affect us at all levels. Spa/salons need to be more aware of the music they play, a fountain's influence with soothing sounds of water, and how employees communicate with each other and clients. Do employees truly *listen* and hear what their clients desire? Can they discern and truly help the client meet their needs?

Chakra #6

The sixth Chakra is the "Third Eye" (Fig. 5–8). Its Sanskrit name is Ajna (to perceive). It has the following qualities:

- Superimposed at the brow area, or the *third eye,* connected to the carotid plexus (sinus)

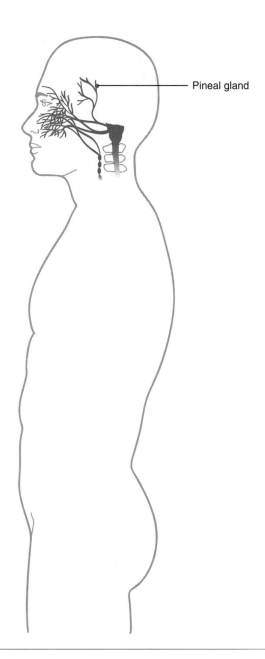

Pineal gland

Figure 5–8   Chakra #6.

- Associated with the following:

  Pineal gland

  Eyes

  Central nervous system

- Associated with the act of seeing, both physically and intuitively—contact between the human mind and the Divine

- Associated with the deep inner level of being we call *spirit,* where our true motivations are

- Balanced energy: lets us *see the big picture,* oriented to self-reflection, forgiveness, and compassion

- Unbalanced energy: headaches, lack of clarity, and difficulty in concentration

- Color: indigo (combination of red/blue)

- Musical note: A

- Gemstone: lapis lazuli, indigo sapphire, quartz

- Element: sense/light

- Essence: jasmine, mint, star anise

- Verb: I see

When we lose our expectations over how things *should be,* we begin to see them as they are. When we see individuals for who they truly are and situations as they truly are, rather than what we want them to *be,* we will feel more serenity. With our intuition, we *see* our way through situations and make constant decisions by discerning what we perceive and organizing the patterns. *We see not with the eye, but with the soul.* We receive information from around us all the time—we see it, hear it, smell it, and sense it.

To expand our consciousness, we must be aware of the constant input of visual and other stimulation. Nourish yourself with beauty whenever you can. Aesthetically beautiful surroundings such as fine art and natural landscapes can rejuvenate us when we are tired. When we learn that what we take in with our eyes is a form of energy, we pay closer attention to its effect on our consciousness and our behavior. Beauty and ambiance in the spa and salon can soothe the soul and renew the body, mind, and spirit. Art principles of color, line design, balance, form, textural combinations, harmony, and rhythm become essential criteria when designing and creating *a healing sanctuary* for your clients.

Chakra #7

The seventh Chakra is the "Crown." Its Sanskrit name is Sahasrara (thousandfold). It has the following qualities:

- Superimposed at the top of the head
- Associated with the following:

  Pituitary gland

  Endocrine system

  Brain

- Associated with our belief systems, both conscious and unconscious
- Represents Universal Truth—*to live in the present moment,* consciousness, is open and calm
- Balanced energy: includes inspiration, wisdom, cosmic consciousness, spirituality, a *oneness with all*—oriented to self-knowledge
- Unbalanced energy: frustration, migraine headaches, stress, worry, and depression
- Color: violet/white
- Musical note: B
- Gemstone: amethyst, diamond, alexandrite
- Element: sense/thought
- Essence: lotus, oilbanum
- Verb: I know

Our belief systems are the rulers of our actions. Through our experiences we build a personal matrix of information within our mind. Our matrix structure becomes our belief system and the ordering principle of our lives. The path of the Chakra—with the kundalini as "the force" of consciousness—rises and descends, changing our personal matrix, each time allowing a greater perception of the whole and a deeper sense of cosmic order. Each time, we respond by reorganizing our lives to match that order. Once we become aware of all this information, we encounter the other component of this phenomenon by knowing what we must understand. In pure layman's terms this is *the "Aha!" experience.*

To understand the experience, we must insert new bits of information correctly into the preexisting matrix, allowing the interpretations of many levels into one. We must let go of old information because understanding requires a constant transcendent level with the focus of attention rising to new and deeper levels of organization. We are drowning in information as a society but are starved for knowledge, or the state of knowing.

We need to question our personal perceptions and knowledge bases when we are in spa/salons. Do you just have information about a lot of things, or do you take the time to gain the education, wisdom, and understanding needed? With so many changes and new emerging world views, are you open to the new information, and are you experiencing and trying some of the new methods? Or do you not take the time and energy to keep abreast and create for your clients the greatest experience they have ever had? If you do not, there are others who will.

Like a rainbow bridge, the Chakras form the connecting channel between body and mind, spirit and matter, past and future. In the dimension of time, Chakras describe stages of life cycles and cultural evolution. The spa/salon culture is going through an incredible metamorphosis and evolution.

Concepts for Consideration

1. How would you explain the underlying reality behind all existence from a scientist's point of view?
2. How would you describe the effect our thoughts and feelings have on our biochemistry?
3. How would you explain the importance of understanding the connection between the Chakra system, endocrine system, and the spinal column?
4. Why is identifying and describing a *vibration frequency* so important in the spa/salon marketplace today and in the future?
5. Why would identifying the processes of diseases and their causes be of relevance to anyone in spa/salon industry?

CHAPTER

Spa/Salon Services and Treatments

Now that we have a more profound understanding of emerging world views including that of body, mind, and spirit, we can see incredible shifts and changes of focus in the spa/salon industry. Facilities that offer services such as beauty treatments, massage, facials, pedicures, wraps, muds, fitness consultation, and personal nurturing now have to face emerging trends that signal changing consumer interests and needs.

Today the focus is shifting from the pampering and beauty aspects to addressing demands for amenities such as antiaging services, therapeutic benefits, wellness, preventive medicine, energy medicine, alternative healing, and spiritual practices—*blending Eastern and Western, ancient and modern, healing approaches*. To stay abreast of the changes, spa/salon owners and staff need to continually educate themselves so they can devise, enhance, and create new treatments and services that holistically integrate body, mind, and spirit. The *body as the temple of the soul* needs to be nurtured, loved, cared for, and respected.

How Safe Are Your Services?

"When the first patient appeared with purplish, pus-filled boils on her legs, the Santa Cruz dermatologist was not overly alarmed—until three more women arrived with the same weeping skin sores below their knees, all having visited the same nail salon. The local health authorities were alerted, but by the time the infection was traced to whirlpool footbaths at a local nail parlor, 109 women—and one man—would be infected with *mycobacterium fortuitum*, a particularly nasty, fast growing microbe that requires months of antibiotic treatment. In some cases, even the drugs did not work, and some women needed skin grafts to repair their scarred and disfigured legs," reported Sharon Kirby in *The National Post.* The footbath boils scare made the pages of the *New England Journal of Medicine.*

All of the clients/victims received the Roman-style footbaths before their pedicures. The infection was caused by the clumps of hair and skin debris that had accumulated behind the screens in the water intakes. Problems also can occur if technicians use unsanitary nail utensils, reuse emery boards or buffers that should be discarded, and pierce fingernails with drill bits.

The **hydrotherapy** (any treatments using water as a primary facilitator) tubs are another area of concern because of the sanitation requirements not only for the surface but also for the jets. In one spa/salon, while a client was relaxing in a hydrotherapy tub as the therapist turned on the jets, she noticed a dark-colored fluid surfacing in the water. Alarmed, she told the therapist only to have her reply, "Oh, that must be some of the mud from the mud treatment of the previous client." It is imperative to educate staff on sanitation, sterilization, and cleaning, then monitor them to make sure it is being done correctly to ensure infection control and client well-being.

Most U.S. states have some form of licensing requirement for nail technicians; in Canada they are largely unregulated. In Ontario, Canada, nail technicians can be certified after completing a course, although in most provinces in Canada no standard educational requirements, official accreditation, or licensing exist.

Spas: A Place to Heal

"Spas and healing centers offer relaxing, effective treatments to promote beauty, healing and well-being. As spa owners become more aware of the deeper need for healing, better treatments will continue to evolve to facilitate healing. Promotion of spa treatments for healthier, more balanced and less stressful individuals will continue to grow. Prevention as a theme will continue to develop, as well as treatments and programs that unfold the full use of human creativity, intelligence, and spiritual awareness. Everyone needs ways to eliminate stress, to reconnect with nature, and establish our own natural health and well-being."

Richard Edison of Innovative Spa Technologies
<www.innovativespa.com>

Richard believes the time is ripe for today's spas to look at Greek traditions and create healing sanctuaries to suit changing consumer tastes. "Our modern spas and healing centers, as did the Asklepeions in ancient times, will continue to have a great significance for the health and well being of people today. Better treatments are continually evolving, as well as total programs for health and well-being," he says.

As multisensory energy beings, we begin our spa experience the moment we enter a facility. The sights, sounds, colors, and scents tantalize our senses and feelings. If **feng shui** (the art of placement that is based on an instinctive and learned understanding of relationships in space) principles and techniques are incorporated in the conception and interior design of a spa/salon, we feel the flow of energy once we are inside. Like a river flows, you want to create the smoothest path possible, enticing the client to want to experience more *than the look or image*. Clients want to *participate* in the experience by booking services and treatments. "Fantasy adventure" and "pleasure revenge," according to Faith Popcorn, are what individuals seek. To reduce stress and anxiety levels, people are turning to mini luxuries and minor indulgences.

As a spa/salon owner, you want to fulfill the desires and needs of your clients, based on your personal spa philosophy. Your personal spa philosophy is a blend of aspects that offer healing—youthful, spiritual, pleasurable, sensual, exotic—encompassing beauty and wellness. A tremendous amount of insight, knowledge, expertise, creativity, and innovation is required to design your services, treatments, and therapies, combined with the energy and magic of continually upgrading them through research and development. Through professionalism, education, integrity, and caring for clients, you can offer them *the newest and the best*.

How about having a clinical herbal therapist (CHT)—someone with great credentials—on staff? A CHT is equivalent to a medical herbalist in the United Kingdom and will have a sound knowledge of the basic health sciences as they relate to herbal medicine, will understand the role that correct nutrition and lifestyle plays in the maintenance of good health, and will be competent in the assessment and treatment of common ailments by natural and complementary means.

Grant Wilson, CPH, with <www.stillpointhealing.com> has a truly remarkable professional background. Grant's educational background includes a four-year program at the Dominion Herbal College in Vancouver B.C., Canada, where his teachers were medical doctors; a one-year program at Grant McEwan College in Edmonton, A.B., in herbology; a three-year program at Prairie Deva College in Edmonton, A.B., where he studied aromatherapy, iridology, and herbology; plus a one-year program at the British Institute of Homeopathy in homotoxicology. Grant uses Chinese tongue analysis, electroacupuncture testing by Voll, and iridology as assessment tools when working with his clients. He takes a picture of the eye and charts the eye to identify the congestion of the lymphatic system, analyzes the glands and organs of the body, and assesses the overall degree of the health of the body. He then suggests a course of treatment using a variety of modalities. Within the Wellness Center that Grant works in, there are a number of therapists that work together, so a client can receive a massage, reflexology, or energy work.

What types of treatments, services, and therapies are you going to offer your clients? How, in fact, can you create signature treatments, services, and therapies to integrate body, mind, and spirit, which everyone desires? You will find a holistic, encompassing array of ideas that you can use to build your personal spa philosophy and dream—and actualize and manifest your customized treatments, services, and therapies. Consciously understanding that *the body is a unified energy field, an integrated whole, where body, mind, and spirit are one* is the starting point to design and build a spa/salon and create the alchemical services, treatments, and therapies. (**Alchemy** is the physical process to convert base metals such as lead to gold; it is an ancient path of **transformation** [a change in structure, appearance, or character] and spiritual purification, which expands the **consciousness** [awareness, cognizance, and knowingness] and develops insight and intuition.) Through wisdom, beauty, and graciousness you can create a sanctuary of ambiance that welcomes your clients.

Light and Color Therapy

A tremendous amount of research has been conducted in the area of color therapy, which shows how colors affect us at psychological and physiologic levels. Color is reflected light; without light, we see nothing. Light comes to us in measurable waves or beams, ranging from very short fluctuations to very long **oscillations** (fluctuating and moving back and forth between two points). All colors of light have specific frequencies and are composed of pure energy.

Light has two spectrums: visible and invisible. The visible spectrum, which constitutes roughly 12 percent of sunlight, displays light like a rainbow when passed through a prism. The invisible spectrum consists of low-frequency infrared rays, which comprise around 80 percent of sunlight, and high-frequency ultraviolet rays, which make up about 8 percent of sunlight.

Infrared Therapy

German physicians have used whole-body infrared therapy for more than 80 years. Infrared energy penetrates tissues down to an inch below the skin and can mobilize toxins from fat cells and increase circulation. This helps eliminate these toxins through perspiration. Normal sweat is composed of almost 99 percent water, whereas sweat induced by infrared therapy is comprised of nearly 85 percent water. Toxins removed from the body through infrared-induced perspiration make up the difference. The result is increased and improved cellular function, enhancing overall health and well-being.

- The benefits and effects of infrared rays are as follows:

   Relief of pain by soothing heat

   Increase in circulation by dilation of blood vessels and increasing formation of new capillaries, which speeds up the healing process by carrying more oxygen and nutrients

   Stimulation of the production of collagen, which is the essential protein used to repair damaged tissue and to replace old tissue

   Decrease in joint stiffness and relief of muscle spasm

   Increase in metabolism of skin cells and other chemical changes within tissue

   Stimulation of perspiration and oil production

Light Therapy

Ultraviolet light rays do not penetrate as deeply as infrared and can be very helpful in the control of acne. The effects of ultraviolet light include an increase in vitamin D and an increase in blood and lymph circulation and tanning of the skin, resulting from stimulation of the pigmentation process in the skin cells. Both visible and invisible light spectrums can be used in *light therapy* (the application of light rays to the skin for the treatment of disorders) or *photorejuvenation* (the application of light rays for a procedure of skin rejuvenation).

Color Therapy

We know that a direct relationship exists between color (light energy) and health (our energy). Light energy stimulates the body's endocrine system, which is connected to our **Chakra** system—consisting of a rainbow of colors with a range of specific frequencies. Each Chakra resonates with a particular color, musical note, essence, and gemstone or crystal. Scientific research has proved that color affects our feelings, behavior, moods, and energy. Red, for instance, can increase blood pressure, body temperature, and heartbeat. Understanding the energetic principles and integrating these principles into the spa/salon culture will be transformational to our clients. Contingent with colors and frequencies, vibrational medicine is about understanding energy and vibration and how they interact with molecular structure and organism balance.

We all have our favorite colors when it comes to dressing and painting a spa/salon. Then there are particular colors that are trendy or in style for a particular season. Working with your artistic architect and spa consultant will allow you to choose colors for the spa/salon to make your clients feel good. Color, line, and design used in the creation of the spa/salon, as well as in furniture, equipment, and décor, are extremely important.

Do not let these decisions be left to chance or decided by your well-meaning friends. Sometimes an excited friend will invite you over to see their new business or home. Remember the moment you passed through the door, you got a strange, uncomfortable feeling about the place? Did you then wonder to yourself, "Are they color blind?" or "Why would they have chosen that color scheme, type of lighting, or decorative motif?" Do not let the same thing happen to you.

Some characteristics of specific colors include the following:

- **Red:** strong, forceful, security, vitality
- **Orange:** fiery, warm, stimulating
- **Green:** harmony, promoting natural growth, renewal, peace
- **Blue:** healing, relaxing, soothing
- **Indigo:** expansive, intuitive
- **Violet:** spiritual aspiration, inspiration
- **Pink:** love, kindness
- **Turquoise:** concentration, strength

There are many shades, tones, and hues of these colors. Taupe, beige, and eggshell all have different bases to create special effects. Tone on tone with different shades can create beautiful effects.

In the salon area, full-spectrum lighting is very important, whereas diffused lighting is more effective in the spa area. You can create beautiful effects with specific colored lights in your rooms. Specific treatments might include natural, organic color in hydrotherapy tubs to benefit the treatment needed by your client. Some hydrotherapy tubs have colors that radiate outward. Special types of glass with changeable filters can also be used in treatments. Also consider various units, designed similar to **Vichy** showers (a water therapy treatment that incorporates a multijet rainbar that is suspended over a wet bed/table and is used in special treatments to bring the body into balance), with a different color for each of the seven heads.

You can find different color light illuminators on the market equipped with seven color lenses (red, orange, yellow, green, blue, violet, and turquoise) and filters made of crystal. Research all the new equipment, supplies, and treatments you might want to use. Maybe someone will create colored muds for treatments. Every time I go to Sedona, Arizona, and see and feel that beautiful red rock, I think of ways to incorporate it into spa treatments. Earthy, mud treatments have a very grounding effect on individuals.

Crystal Therapy

Interest in **crystal therapies,** an ancient healing art, is also growing. "Crystals have played important roles in many scientific discoveries which have begun to revolutionize the way we think about the structure of consciousness and the universe itself," says Richard Gerber in *Vibrational Medicine.* For instance, a ruby crystal was a key component in the first laser developed by Bell Laboratory scientists in the early 1960s. It has only been within the last century that the knowledge of electromagnetism has given humanity the ability to explore potential healing applications and other beneficial gifts of the crystals and gems, which grow naturally within the earth.

The mineral kingdom has its own expression of **divine energy** (active life force) that can be used for special treatments. For example, quartz crystals can be used for cleansing and balancing Chakras. Patricia Jean Edge, the founder of *Crystal Light Therapy* (pjedge@hotmail.com), introduced her holistic crystal healing massage to the Spa at Las Venturas in Los Cabos, California. Her treatment begins with an ancient ritual of purification called smudging, followed by placing crystals on the energy centers of the body. "By vibrating the crystals through the process of *toning,* one is able to experience and perceive one's light body," says Patricia, whose client base consists of doctors, nurses, lawyers, judges, and movie stars—all individuals aware of their need to use a variety of resources for balance.

"The crystal is a neutral object whose inner structure exhibits in a state of perfection and balance," says crystal researcher Marcel Vogel, a senior scientist who has been with IBM for 27 years. "When it's cut to the proper form and when the human mind enters into relationship with its structural perfection, the crystal emits a vibration that extends and amplifies the powers of the user's mind. Like a laser, it radiates energy in a coherent, highly concentrated form, and this energy may be transmitted into objects or people at will."

Dr. Dolores Krieger, the originator of *Therapeutic Touch,* works with enhancing healing energies through using quartz crystals. If you are interested in exploring crystal therapy, investigate the subject further by reading, checking the Internet, and personally experiencing the therapy. If you choose to incorporate this modality of therapy, send your spa personnel out for training and education.

Music Therapy

Modern science is confirming the ancient wisdom that *music is medicine for the body, mind, and spirit.*

> *"Music sets up a certain vibration which unquestionably results in a physical reaction. Eventually, the proper vibration for every person will be found and utilized."*
>
> George Gershwin

Sound, like light, travels in waves through the air and is measured in frequencies and in intensities. **Sound frequency** refers to pitch—the high or low quality of sounds—and is measured in **hertz (Hz),** the number of cycles per second at which the wave vibrates. The lower the pitch, the slower the vibration; the higher the pitch, the faster the vibration. The research of Dr. Alfred Tomatis has established the healing and creative powers of sound and music.

Some of music's therapeutic effects include the following:

- Brain waves can slow down and equalize by music and self-generated sounds. Certain baroque and New Age music can shift consciousness from **beta waves** (brain waves present when the nervous system is active and when there is sensory input and mental activity; waves with a frequency of 14 to 30 Hz) to **alpha waves** (brain waves present when normal individuals are awake in a resting state; waves with a frequency of 8 to 13 Hz), which enhance well-being and alertness. Mozart or baroque music helps focus conscious awareness and increase mental organization.

- Breathing deepens and slows down, which is what allows the mind to calm down with Gregorian chants and New Age music.

- Heartbeat, pulse rate, and blood pressure are lowered with easy listening and softer music.

- Stress hormones in the blood decline significantly when listening to relaxing, soft music.

■ Current research claims insufficient oxygen in the blood can be a major cause of immune deficiency and degenerative disease. The *Mozart Effect* claims certain types of music, as well as singing and chanting, can actually oxygenate the cells.

■ Olav Skille, a Norwegian, devised a musical bath, known as vibroacoustic therapy, wherein youngsters were immersed in a range of sound: New Age, ambient, classical, and popular music reduced muscle tension and improved body movement and coordination. Vibroacoustic therapy increased the range of movement in individual's spines, arms, hips, and legs. Music in the lower frequencies—between 40 and 66 Hz—resonates in the lower back region, pelvis, thighs, and legs, whereas higher frequency music is felt more in the upper chest, neck, and head.

■ Endorphin levels can increase with music, which induces a natural high and reduces pain.

■ Perception of time changes with specific musical selections. Classical and baroque music provokes orderly behavior, whereas highly romantic or New Age music softens stressful situations and seems to make time stand still.

■ Productivity increases with the type of music listened to. A University of Washington study concluded that accuracy in copy editing a manuscript by 90 individuals who listened to classical music for 90 minutes increased by 21.3 percent. In contrast, those listening to a popular commercial radio station improved by only 2.4 percent.

■ Dr. George Lozanov's methods have been used to enhance memory through music.

■ A sense of well-being and safety can be created by music that provides a sanctuary for the listener.

Given the power of music, we need to be more aware of our choices of motifs in the spa/salon. With some creativity, innovation, and an understanding of music, you can come up with applicable treatments, services, and therapies that include specific musical selections.

If the power of music and its effects on body, mind, and spirit appeal to you, research, study, and experiment with different music selections.

Aromatherapy

Inhaled smells act on the sensitive olfactory nerves in the nose and rapidly transmit the message to the brain, which resends that message to other parts of the body. **Aromacology** (the study of aromas) and **aromatherapy** (the application of that knowledge) are based on the principles of ayurveda—a type of medicine practiced in India for more than 5,000 years that identifies a person's constitution and treats the person with diet, exercise, meditation, herbs, massage, sun, and breathing to bring harmony to the physical, mental, and spiritual health of the individual. Many ancient cultures in Egypt, China, Persia, Greece, and Rome used pressed flowers to create healing remedies and natural medicines. Research has since rediscovered the powerful effects (antiviral, antibacterial, antifungal, hormonal, oxygenating, and uplifting) of essential oils, used by aromatherapists as ingredients in creams, lotions, sprays, massage oils, and bath oils or as vapors. Aromatherapists are also concerned with psychological and physiologic effects of aromas on individuals.

Everything in the universe is a manifestation of *yin* and *yang*, which are two opposite energies attracting and balancing each other. It is essential to maintain a balance of these energies in the body and mind. For example, if a hot or stimulated condition (yang) exists, cooling or calming (yin) properties may be used to balance this condition. This balancing practice, through the use of opposites, can also apply to balancing ourselves physiologically and psychologically. Each plant and flower essence is dominant in either of the yin and yang extremes, as are the psychological conditions of the mind. Once the message of the essence has been communicated to the brain through the olfactory system (smell), a reaction is stimulated via the sympathetic and parasympathetic nervous systems, resulting in a corresponding psychological and physiologic reaction. The messages may have either a stimulating or calming effect on a variety of conditions. In many cases, it can have both effects, leaving one alert and calm, thus balancing the existing condition.

Flowers and herbs are especially pure and potent sources of yin and yang energies. A plant in full bloom is at the peak of its growth, and the life force **(prana** or **chi)** in a flowering plant is in its most active and potent state. A plant's life force is a unique combination of properties known as the **absolute essence.** The absolute essence gives flowers and plants their individual aromas, which have different effects on us psychologically and physiologically. In their purest state, these essences function as natural remedies because they reestablish mental and physical balance.

The absolute essence is present in the plant in the form of invisible molecular gases. In aromatherapy, plants are harvested in full bloom and put through a special distillation process. Through evaporation and distillation, the absolute essence of the plant is extracted in liquid form, and the natural properties are obtained at their highest level of purity and potency. In this way, the plant's life force lives on in potent form even after its flowers have died. This is why natural essences have such a revitalizing effect. We can feel and even see the physical and mental energy that comes from these pure, natural sources. What we are actually seeing and feeling is the vital life force released in its purest form.

The Egyptians, who were among the earliest practitioners of aromatherapy, vaporized floral and herbal oils in small pots of boiling water to soften the skin, soothe the mind, and normalize the functions of the various glands in the body. Ayurvedic medical texts even specified which oils were used for each gland.

There is a tremendous difference between a pure, natural product and a confection with merely some natural ingredients. If only a small fraction of a product's ingredients come from natural sources, it is not really natural. To determine which products are natural, read the ingredient list. If the first ingredient and second ingredients are derived from a natural source, the product is pure and natural. Otherwise, if natural ingredients appear third or fourth in the list, the word natural has been misused. Synthetic products tend to irritate the nervous system by upsetting its delicate balance. If natural essences are absent in the formula, these products do not carry any vital life force, and without the life force, no revitalizing effects exist. Synthetic aromas are manufactured in laboratories with gasoline byproducts. These artificial essences do not carry nature's organic molecular structure or the therapeutic benefits of natural aromas.

Organically certified is an important term that claims the botanical raw materials are grown on certified organic farms. This assures consumers that no petrochemical fertilizers or pesticides have been used on the farm or during handling or processing.

You may also want to check out a few aromas, which could brighten your facility. Lavender has equal qualities of yin and yang. Rose is considered the queen of essential oils, and jasmine is considered the king. Remember that aromatherapy is considered a **vibrational energy medicine**—or an **essence energy** (the active force of a substance distilled or extracted from another substance)—and can be sprayed in treatment rooms; put in a diffuser in treatment rooms; used in steam therapy, hydrotherapy tubs, and facial steams; and added to massage oil.

The greatest challenge in the spa/salon industry is attracting and retaining educated, knowledgeable staff capable of administering aromatherapy. Some individuals will read a book or take a one-day class and pass themselves off as experts. Aromatherapy courses can range from six months to seven years, depending on the school and certification. Work with a company with excellent training and educational support. Staff should also be well versed on the oils applied during the treatment.

Fortunately, aromatherapy is getting some serious academic and educational consideration. Elizabeth Jones, director of the College of Botanical Healing Arts in Santa Cruz, California, and the owner of Elizabeth Van Buren Essential Oils, trains aromatherapists in the cellular, spiritual, and emotional levels of essential oil use. British author, aromatherapist, and educator Shirley Price claims, "Lavender angustifolia can have the same effects as the depression drug Prozac—raising low **serotonin** (a neurotransmitter in the brain) levels in the brain—with no side effects."

Professor Paolo Rovesti, with the help of the University of Milan in Italy, studied aroma and its emotional reflex. The study measured pulse rate, blood pressure, and respiration in relationship to each of two groups of aromatics, one thought to be stimulating and the other sedative. The project concluded that lemon, peppermint, cedar, cinnamon, and ylang ylang stimulated the body, whereas Melissa, Roman chamomile, and neroli had sedative effects.

Raindrop Therapy

Spa/salon owners and personnel should look into *raindrop therapy,* a specialized massage with essential oils. Raindrop therapy originated almost two decades ago, a result of collaborative research between Dr. D. Gary Young and a Lakota medicine man. The therapy integrates Vita-Flex (a massage technique/stroke) and massage therapy with essential oils to bring the body into structural and electrical alignment.

Raindrop therapy is based on the theory that many types of **scoliosis** (a physical finding in which curvature of the spine is present) and spinal misalignments are caused by viruses or bacteria that lie dormant along the spine. These pathogens create inflammation, which, in turn, controls and disfigures the spinal column. In raindrop therapy, specified oils are sequentially dispensed like little drops of rain 6 inches above the back and massaged along the vertebrae. The oils continue to work in the body for 5 to 7 days following a treatment, with continued realignment taking place during this time.

Valor, the most important oil used in this treatment, works on both physical and emotional levels, supporting the electrical and energy alignments of the body. The key to using the blend of oils is patience. Once the frequencies begin to balance in these areas, a structural alignment can occur. For more information, check out <www.youngliving.com> or call (800) 282-8702. Research this therapy; and personally experience it. If you are interested, get your staff members educated and trained.

Water Treatment

Researching methods of water treatment for your spa/salon can be confusing. Have you ever wondered if the chemicals and minerals in your water affect the beneficial ingredients of your spa/salon services and treatments? After talking with several companies, I chose an objective and knowledgeable authority on the subject: Dale Armistead, a journeyman plumber certified in water treatment for residential, commercial, and agricultural systems.

"Without water we would have no world. No living organism can exist long without it. Water is one of Mother Nature's greatest gifts and makes up approximately 81 percent of all living matter. For every 10 pounds of the human body, seven pounds is water.

Purifying water is nothing new, however. Archeologists studying ancient Egyptian culture have discovered that around 3000 BC, government officials called vizars *were required to inspect the water supply of the entire land every 10 days. We also know they were aware of disinfecting water through boiling, filtration, distillation, and clarification of water by coagulation—techniques still used today. In the seventeenth century, France and England used* **chlorine** *(a nonmetallic element that is found alone as a strong-smelling, greenish–yellow irritating gas that is used as a bleach, oxidizing agent, and disinfectant) to treat water, which is another process still used.*

To determine the appropriate water for whatever purpose, an individual must consider the analysis and the use of the water. That is why in today's society, with our chemicals and sewage, raw water analysis is so important for water to be treated safely and economically. Before we look at water treatment, we must first assess the nature of the water, the chemicals, and the amount of contaminants or impurities. To make it simpler, we have created general water quality requirements:

1. Free of disease-producing organisms

2. Colorless, clear, odorless, and tasteless

3. Noncorrosive and free of gases and staining minerals

Impure water may contain waterborne diseases such as typhoid fever, cholera, and dysentery; it also may contain water viruses such as polio, jaundice, hepatitis, and—worst of all—cysts and amoebic dysentery. All of these can be controlled by chlorine, which must be used in higher concentrations for longer retention times in attacking viruses that cause cysts. Water must also contain dissolved minerals, gases, sediment, color, organic matter, taste, odor, and other microorganisms.

Classes of Water

Surface water is usually slightly acidic, corrosive, and relatively soft. There is a popular belief that spring water is pure, sparkling, and clear, but it actually contains large amounts of minerals, high levels of turbidity (such as sand and other particles), and large amounts of bacteria. Ground water is usually higher in mineral content, but it is usually filtered well through all the different levels of soil, sand, and gravel that it passes through.

Water Criteria

The general maximum level for sodium is 300 parts per million (PPM). With 500 to 700 PPM, you get an unpleasant taste. Individuals on sodium-restricted diets should have their water analyzed. Reverse osmosis, demineralization, or distillation may remove sodium.

Water in Alberta, Canada, rarely has potassium levels higher than 20 PPM. Levels registering more than 2,000 PPM are harmful to the nervous system.

Calcium is one cause of water hardness, with acceptable limits of 200 PPM. It makes water unsuitable for laundry and bathing. It also causes dry skin and scaling in kettles, coffee makers, and water heaters.

Magnesium is the other cause of water hardness. A limit of 150 PPM for taste consideration is suggested.

Iron levels as low as 0.2 to 0.3 PPM will cause staining of laundry and plumbing fixtures, whereas 1 to 2 PPM has a metallic taste. Iron has not been known to be hazardous to people's health.

Sulfates (or SO^4) readings at more than 500 PPM produce a laxative effect in humans and animals, whereas 650 to 700 PPM adds to the effect with a medicinal taste. Sulfates recorded at very high levels have been associated with some brain disorders in cattle and pigs. Removal of sulfates also can be accomplished by using reverse osmosis, demineralization, and distillation.

The maximum level of chloride is 250 PPM, whereas nitrates (NO^2) should be no more than 1 PPM. Nitrates are indicators of direct contamination by sewers as well as fertilizers and seepage from dumpsites. Nitrites (NO^3), which cause irritation of stomach and bladders if digested by humans, should not be higher than 10 PPM.

Desired levels for fluoride are 1.5 PPM. Levels of more than 1.5 PPM may cause tooth mottling and will cause dark brown stains of the teeth.

The pH (potential of hydrogen and a measure of acidity or alkalinity) balance of water between 6.5 and 8.5 is acceptable, with 7 being neutral. Adding limestone chips or mixing soda ash with a feed pump can alter the pH balance.

Water Ratio/Hardness		*Table 6–1*
Soft	0–50 PPM	
Moderately soft	50–100 PPM	
Moderately hard	100–200 PPM	
Hard	200–400 PPM	
Very hard	400–600 PPM	
Extremely hard	Over 600 PPM	

Water Treatment Process

Iron Removal

1. *Water softener: Less than 3 PPM ferric/ferrous substances will be removed. The filter bed must be backwashed thoroughly, which could cause problems on an acreage as a result of too much wastewater.*

2. *Manganese-zeolite filter: Removes up to 10 PPM of ferric/ferrous iron. One drawback to this system is magnesium permanganate must always be added; it is messy to work with and will also kill your septic field.*

3. *Colloidal type iron filter: Requires no chemicals, and removes up to 25 PPM of ferric/ferrous iron. However, if your water contains sulfur or tannins, these will foul up the filter bed.*

4. *Chlorination: Recommended when the water contains sulphur, extreme iron bacteria. When taste and odor exists in the water, a chlorine injection must be followed by a sand filter to catch sediment and an activated carbon filter to remove excess chlorine.*

5. *Air injection: removes up to 30 PPM of ferric/ferrous iron*

Sulphur Removal

1. *Aeration: Recommended only after water analysis*

2. *Manganese-zeolite filters: Removal of up to 5 PPM, although you have to deal with messy chemicals that could also kill a field septic system*

3. *Chlorinating: Must be followed by a sand filter and then by an activated carbon filter*

Corrosive Removal

1. *Neutralizing filter with limestone chips*

2. *Soda ash by a feed pump*

Turbidity Removal

Turbidity removal involves chlorinating, followed by a sand filter then by an activated carbon filter.

Taste and Odor Removal

Taste and odors may be removed by installation of an activated carbon filter, which can be used to remove chlorine.

Reverse Osmosis Units

Reverse osmosis (RO) units remove a wide variety of contaminates and impurities but not all of them. RO units are sold as the miracle filter, but in reality, they require a lot of pretreatment. They also require an optimum temperature of $25°C$, so you must install retention tanks to raise water temperature.

RO units require costly pretreatment:

1. Iron and manganese (maximum 1 PPM)

2. Iron bacteria must be controlled

3. Water must be soft

4. Chlorine levels must be closely controlled

5. Clean water, mineral sediment

6. pH level between 5 and 8

7. Total dissolved solids less than 1,500 PPM

Household RO units waste up to 5 to 8 L of water for every single level of purified water. In most cases, a water distiller is more practical and economical. You should have your water tested every year by contacting your public health unit.

With today's technology we have many ways of disinfecting our drinking water:

1. Boiling

2. Ultraviolet light

3. Chlorine

4. **Ozone** (a bluish gaseous reactive form of oxygen that is formed naturally in the atmosphere and is used for disinfecting, deodorizing, and bleaching; pure and refreshing air) treatment

5. Solar distillation

When using chlorine, all systems should have sand filters followed by an activated carbon filter. Ultraviolet light units require a sand filter and an activated carbon filter.

Dale Armitstead

Water Therapy

Hippocrates, a big proponent of steam bathing, praised its virtues by saying, "Give me the power to create a fever, and I shall cure any disease." A part of hydrotherapeutic tradition in European and American Spas, **sweat therapy,** is used to prepare for massages to increase suppleness of the muscles and create a deep sense of relaxation in the body and mind (Fig. 6–1).

Mayo Clinic research has found that the number of white blood cells increased by an average of 58 percent during artificially induced fever brought on by steam. Chinese medicine views sweating as one of three methods to rid the body of bad chi—the misdirected energy thought to be responsible for disease. Dr. John Webes, director of the College of Massage Therapy in Omaha, Nebraska, recommends **steam therapy** in the treatment of cellulite, finding it superior to body wraps in raising temperature.

Steam room, which prepares client for a massage.   *Figure 6–1*

When people feel tired, or just want their minds to drift, their natural instinct is to take solace. Alternating hot and cold footbaths increases circulation in the legs and feet. Have two containers ready—one with hot water and the other with cold water—making sure the water level is above the ankles. This is also an excellent treatment for varicose veins.

Hydrotherapy has been documented for thousands of years—from the ruins of ancient baths found in Greece and Rome to artifacts found next to mineral pools in every part of the world. The modern history of hydrotherapy starts with thermal therapy: the mystical capacities of hot springs around the world. Studies have concluded that lactic acid in the muscles can be released when certain ingredients are used in a hydrotherapy tub soak. Under certain conditions, skin can absorb substances; specific tub treatments have minerals and ingredients that become active.

Having a specialized soak after a massage stops the aching muscles, whereas specific ingredients in a hydrotherapy tub soak can help ease inflammation and pain in certain chronic disorders, including arthritis, rheumatism, and fibromyalgia. The jets of the hydrotherapy tub can activate certain ingredients and have a therapeutic effect on the body. A relaxing soak soothes the body, mind, and spirit. Consider adding specific essential oils and an element of color therapy, such as colored water or colored lights, to create a mood and enhance the therapeutic effects.

Are you looking at transforming your spa into a piece of art? One product shows how *bathing in light and music* adds that extra edge, using water in new dimensions of listening and relaxing. German multimedia artist Micky Remann developed the "liquid sound" concept and installation after getting the idea from musical interactions with wild Orca whales in the Pacific Northwest. His concept became a key element in Taskana-Therme Bad Sulza, a futuristic spa complex that features seven pools of multimedia, sound, and light and was registered at Expo 2000 in Germany as one of the event's first world projects. Anyone who has ever swum with dolphins or heard the music of whales can attest to this indescribable, awesome experience.

Thalassotherapy means treatment by seawater and marine climate, bringing all abundant water (iodine, sulfur, calcium, and mineral salts) into the body through the skin. Marine elements pass through the skin in baths at a 35°C (98°F) temperature.

"Scientific proof of minerals and trace elements found in seawater are indeed absorbed through the skin," says Dr. Yves Tréguer, president of the Fédération Internationale de al Thalassothérapie Mer et Santé, founded in 1986. "People taking antiinflammatory drugs don't need them after seaside treatments. Others find they no longer require sleeping pills."

The effects of hydrotherapy are reinforced by algae therapy, a seaweed collection treatment. We can use seaweed soaks in hydrotherapy tubs or seaweed wraps because obviously we do not have the sea or the climate. Total or partial body seaweed wraps slim down, remineralize, detoxify, and relax the body. The cosmetic product's quality depends on the caliber of the raw materials. Thoroughly research the product line before using them in spa treatments. Marine treatments work on the skin's surface, and others penetrate more deeply.

Water therapies include pools, baths, steam showers, body wraps, and transdermal treatments that remineralize the system. Modalities we can use in spa/salons include the following:

- **Hydrotherapy**—treatments using temperature and pressure
- **Balneotherapy**—systematic application of mineral water
- **Thalassotherapy**—involving seawater and sea products
- **Steam therapy**—treatments using steam
- **Body wraps** and/or **hydrating therapies**—treatments using gauze or cheesecloth

To reap the benefits of thalassotherapy's specific treatments, services, and products, it is important to update spa standards by adopting therapies based on positive results from sound scientific studies instead of relying on spa folklore. A good start would be to have some basic understanding of marine spa substances and their therapeutic properties (see box).

There are some amazing cosmetics and treatment products using the science of **phytotherapy,** which uses the unscented parts of botanicals, such as vitamins, minerals, amino acids, proteins, and enzymes.

Body Care

We have some amazing cosmetic products to perform specific body treatments, services, and therapies. They are explained in the following paragraphs.

Skin Brushing

- **Skin brushing** is a powerful therapy that affects the entire body, considering the skin is a major organ.
- The Japanese used vigorous skin brushing with loofah sponges before their traditional hot bath.
- Greek athletes used *strigiles*—specialized spoonlike scrapers after training sessions—before bathing.

ACTIVE INGREDIENT AND THERAPEUTIC ACTION

- Laminaria algae

Energy concentrate with 60 minerals and vitamins

Basic treatment that restores and balances energy

- Fucus algae

Slimming concentrate containing more than 60 diverse trace elements

Eliminates toxins through perspiration

Remarkable thermostatic properties

- Laminaria combined with marine sediment

Purifying ocean clay with strong thermostatic action

Absorbs impurities through the skin

Hydrating of the skin

- Lithothamnium algae combined with laminaria

High concentrates of calcium, magnesium, iron, and manganese provide cellular energy to muscles; increase blood oxygenation; and restore equilibrium

Increases general metabolism

- Spirulina algae combined with laminaria

High protein and vitamin content regenerate dermal and epidermal skin tissue and improve elasticity and tone

Hydrating and revitalizing action on the skin

- Cherokee Indians used dried corncobs to enhance the skin.
- Comanche Indians used sand from Texas river bottoms to scrub their skin.
- Actual brushes with a handle and natural fiber bristles are used.

Benefits

- Causes **exfoliation,** or dead skin cell removal (cellular buildup takes place with aging because cellular renewal is slower)
- Increases lymph and blood circulation
- Stimulates oil and sweat glands
- Stimulates the vital chi moving through the body's meridians
- Helps to increase and regenerate production of collagen and elastin fibers

- Leads to rosy-looking, youthful, and resilient skin
- Can help alleviate cellulite

There are many types of body wraps (Fig. 6–2), muds, masks, parafango, firming, toning, sculpting, and so on. We have some excellent cosmetic companies. Do your research and make sure you have excellent training and support.

Self-tanning (a product that darkens the skin when applied) and ***self-bronzing*** (a product that gives the skin a bronze color when applied) offer large market prospects for the spa/salon industry. However, most facilities face some specific challenges such as stained sheets, hands, and towels from the products as well as insufficient products for moisturizing and home maintenance. St. Tropez Tanning Essentials <www.sttropeztan.com> is definitely an upscale and professional company that provides customers with a complete line of tanning essentials. The company has an incredible line of eight tanning items formulated with the highest quality ingredients available in today's market and accessories developed in response to requests from their European distributors and the spa industry. The impressive tanning accessories and items—such as a fitted table cover (black), bath sheet

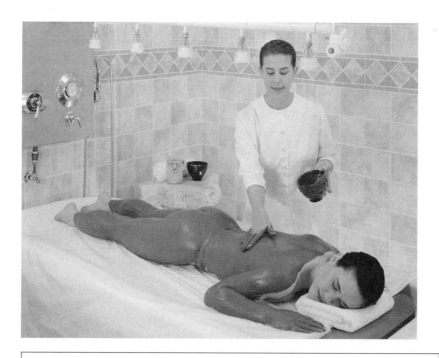

A mud treatment.   *Figure 6–2*

BODY TREATMENTS HAVE EXTRAORDINARY BENEFITS

- Encourages cellular renewal
- Activates cellular metabolism
- Helps renewal of epidermal cells
- Reduces the *orange peel* cellulite by diminishing fatty deposits
- Draws out toxins and stimulates circulation in tissue
- Stimulates lymphatic flow in the body to draw out toxins from around cells
- Helps lift flabby buttocks and breasts, flattens the abdomen, and contours the figure
- Tones and firms the entire body
- Activates the surface circulation and increases elasticity of the skin
- Revitalizes the skin and improves surface smoothness
- Remineralizes and relieves muscular pain
- Rejuvenates, oxygenates cells, and moisturizes the skin
- Refines the silhouette by activating the natural process of excess fatty deposit elimination
- Relieves stress and fatigue, and makes you feel good
- May provide pain relief (touch is emotionally nurturing and caring)

(black), modesty towel (black), satin gloves (black), terry cloth headbands (black), turbans (black), tanning mitts (white), and disposable thongs (black) add a touch of elegance to the spa. When someone comes in to have tanning service, it is easy to offer them a body exfoliant or body treatment as they naturally work together.

There are some incredible new tanning systems out in the marketplace, so do your research and find out if the investment will reap the profits you expect. Check out the airbrushing systems for tanning and makeup and try some of the new lay down and stand up tanning beds.

Facials

Everyone wants to have healthy, radiant, blemish-free, youthful skin. Facials improve the skin's tone, texture, and elasticity and can refine lines.

Again, there are many excellent cosmetic companies. Experiment, do your research, and check educational opportunities and product and service support. Samples are popular items that you can provide clients so they can experiment with them at home.

Retail sales are so important because home maintenance products are necessary to keep your clients' skin looking and feeling great. Rehydration, cellular renewal, and line-refining qualities are important aspects of skin care. Also important is vitamin therapy, especially vitamin C, which has oxygenating aspects that are instrumental in improving your skin.

The same emphasis we place on revitalizing the skin on our faces should also go into our hands and feet. Time and time again, I have seen individuals who have had facelifts, but their hands give away their true age. Men are frequenting the spa more nowadays and are interested in services and treatments (Fig. 6–3). Once a man experiences a facial, he usually is very dedicated in using the home maintenance products he has purchased.

Antiaging Treatments

Antiaging products and treatments are in great demand in the marketplace today, and there are many extremely great lines available. Research and experiment with the many products on the market. Stefania Anderson,

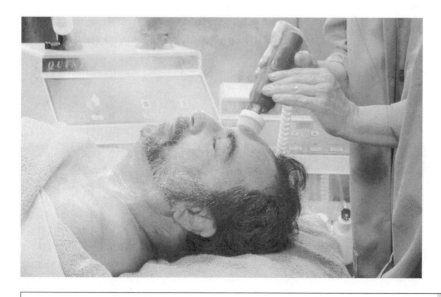

Men's facials are becoming very popular.   *Figure 6–3*

founder of a progressive cosmetic company Amore Skin Sense, had a philosophy and a dream about skin care and makeup products that would go beyond tradition into the realm of antiaging *cosmeceuticals*. In the 1990s, she set out to create state-of-the-art, highly effective skin treatment products that would not only successfully combine natural ingredients with the latest scientific technology but also provide aestheticians and doctors the tools required to address all their clients' needs.

Back then, such an ambition was a major challenge. The aesthetic industry was only vaguely aware of alpha hydroxy acids (AHA) and was leery about trying new active products and techniques. Thanks to a core group of trailblazers in the aesthetic and medical field, her company carved a niche with products such as epidermal growth factor (EGF), glycolic acid polymer, antioxidants, and vitamins for the skin.

Stefania's next challenge came with the invention of a healthy alternative to traditional makeup (Micronized Mineral Makeup). "Natural mineral pigments from the earth eliminated the need for chemical dyes or preservatives, which mostly contribute to allergic reactions. The minerals allow the skin to breathe and function normally while providing full-spectrum sun protection and a natural antiinflammatory," says Stefania. After an invasive aesthetic treatment such as peels, microdermabrasion, and laser surgery (after open lesions heal), this makeup line can be used to protect the skin from sun and airborne pollutants.

Preoccupation with therapies to reduce aging is growing dramatically. Homeopathic medicine and therapies are also increasingly popular and could rival plastic surgery as an antiaging alternative. Some people are spending up to $800 a month for injections, and laser treatments are rapidly becoming as popular as leg waxing and facials. Refer your client to a laser specialist if you do not have a doctor on staff.

Oxygen Therapy

There are many types of **oxygen therapy,** from oxygen bars to hyperbarics. Oxygen delivered farther and deeper into the cells and tissues, after being dissolved into the circulatory system and body fluids, promotes cellular healing. Check with your local health board before providing oxygen in your facility. Not only are oxygen tanks highly combustible, the Food and Drug Administration officially recognizes oxygen as a drug, which must be authorized by a physician. There are even specialized oxygen-therapy skin care product lines in the marketplace.

Massage and Bodywork

More than 2,000 years ago, the Chinese practice of manipulating pressure points provided the first written reference to bodywork, whereas knowledge of spinal column adjustment through massage was described in an ancient Egyptian papyrus from 1,700 BC. Bodywork and massage allow us to explore our body, mind, and spirit and shift our focus from *thinking* to *experiencing* and *feeling*. It includes traditional massage and other approaches to working with the body.

Psychologists are realizing the power of getting in touch with the body. "It is now obvious to me that although it was never said, my education clearly suggested that the brain was the most important aspect of my physical being, that it controlled the body, and that it should be in control," says Anne Wilson Schaef in *Beyond Therapy, Beyond Science.* "There was no real recognition that the body, too, can remember, that feelings are necessary to the brain, that the brain needs the body for full information, and that the memories and feelings stored in the body are in most instances more accurate than those stored in the brain. What a revelation it was in this work to see that the body often is the seat of the most clearly stored information and that the only way to fully participate in our lives is to use our bodies, brains, feelings, intuitions, awareness, and thoughts. In order to fully participate in our lives and in our world, we had to be in our bodies and open to the information that is stored there. Clarity comes from doing our deep process work."

In the United States, massage was practiced in hospitals and included in physical therapy until the 1950s, when it evolved into a separate discipline. Later that decade, the space race spurred a scientific movement in popular culture, while advances in surgery and antibiotics swayed conventional belief that modern medicine could cure any illness. As a result, massage declined in popularity until the 1970s, when growth of the human potential movement rekindled interest in the practice. The Office of Alternative Medicine was established in 1992 by the U.S. Congress to evaluate complementary health care practices; within a year, bodywork projects were awarded the lion's share of research grants. Several different types of massage and bodywork treatments corresponding to different philosophies are available, although education and certification of each classification will vary.

Massage happens to be the most popular spa treatment according to the majority of the research (Fig. 6–4). Body treatments are an excellent addition for the client before or after the massage, depending on the specific requirements of the product line you are using.

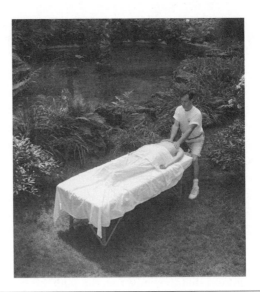

| *Figure 6–4* | Touch in massage triggers the body's natural healing response. |

Some very basic protocol considerations to remember when doing massage are as follows:

- Present yourself professionally—free of body and breath odors
- Have a clean, neat room with a comfortable temperature
- Ask the client if they prefer soothing music or a quiet background
- Soft diffused lighting creates ambiance
- Fill in the client consultation form, and discuss their personal concerns
- Check if they have medical benefits that cover a portion of the massage
- Choose your massage oil, lotion, or creme with care; mineral oils are not recommended because of the petroleum base that clogs the pores and dries the skin

Swedish Massage

Swedish massage has the following characteristics:

- Basic therapeutic approach to healing, which incorporates a variety of massage strokes to the soft-tissue structure

- Helps the body remove toxins and deliver nutrients to tissues and cells more quickly

- Helps recover from strains and trauma more quickly

Sports massage, a specialty area of traditional massage, helps achieve maximum physical performance and protects against pain and injuries.

Rolfing

Rolfing has the following characteristics:

- Structural integration is a technique of manipulating the soft tissue of the body to restore flexibility and ease of movement by freeing segments of the body, which become locked in patterns of tension.

- *Deep tissue massage* or bodywork focuses on the myofascial system.

- To be aligned vertically, a plumb line dropped from an individual's head to feet should form a straight line, passing through the midpoints of five key landmarks: the ears, shoulder joints, hip joints, knees, and ankles.

- Rolfing protocol includes having your photo taken before and after each session to chart the progress of change.

- Rolfing series follows a systematic process that reflects progression to restructure the body.

Alexander Technique

The Alexander technique involves the following:

- It is a system of aligning the spine and reeducating your body and mind.

- Key body relationships include the head, neck, and torso.

- The neck is of prime importance because it is the area through which all the nerves that receive sensory input from, and direct motor activity to nearly the entire body.

- All the vertebrae of the spinal column are interconnected through a series of complex joints; pressure on the neck vertebrae can cause pressure throughout the rest of the vertebral column. This results in pressure on nerve roots as they exit the spinal column, causing pain, aches, and contracted muscles.

- North American Society of Teachers of the Alexander Technique (NASTAT) has established standards, training, and certification of teachers.

Feldenkrais Method

The Feldenkrais method has two formats:

- One-on-one private lessons called functional integration, wherein through touch, the body communicates new and efficient methods of movement

- Awareness Through Movement, a group class where a teacher verbally guides students through a structured sequence of movement explorations.

The objective is to bring unconscious movement into conscious awareness and provide options that enable us to choose patterns of movement and behavior. The Feldenkrais training program is generally conducted over a period of 4 years, with several intensive sessions of several weeks each year.

Myofascial Release

Myofascial release has the following characteristics:

- It is a whole-body approach to healing that seeks to restore balance to the body by releasing tension in the fascia. Fascia is a thin layer system of connective tissue that supports, surrounds, and interweaves every organ, muscle, and bone in the body.

- Along with release of physical tension, clients report a release of emotional material.

- When energy has been blocked, or locked in a place and is released, heat is given off.

- It is especially effective for longer-term relief of chronic pain and dysfunction associated with muscular tightness—including neck, jaw, and back pain; muscle tension; and stress-related disorders.

- There is no separate national licensing for myofascial release. It is taught in a series of intensive, sequential workshops to health professionals who already have licenses or certificates in related disciplines.

Trager Approach

The Trager approach has the following characteristics:

- Reeducates the nervous system in more relaxed, less painful patterns.

- A typical psychophysical integration includes gentle rhythmic rocking, kneading, shaking, vibrating, and stretching movements to increase range of motion and induce relaxation.

- Trager practitioners are trained and certified by the Trager Institute in Mill Valley, California.

Rubenfeld Synergy Method

The Rubenfeld Synergy method has the following characteristics:

- It combines touch with verbal expression to promote healing and unify body, mind, emotions, and spirit.

- Gentle touch, verbal expression, and movement detect areas of emotional holding and tension.

- It includes training in the Alexander technique, the Feldenkrais method, Gestalt practice, and Ericksonian hypnotherapy.

- A **synergist** uses a gentle touch, which is not invasive and does not inflict pain, to encourage a client to a more pleasurable way of being.

Rosen Method

The Rosen method has the following characteristics:

- It is an approach to healing that uses gentle touch and verbal support to assist clients in unlocking old memories that can prevent them from *becoming* or realizing their full potential.

- In letting go of suppressed emotions, individuals report a release of chronic muscular tension.

- Breath is the gateway between the unconscious and the conscious.

- Training includes intensive training plus a clinical internship.

Shiatsu

Shiatsu has the following characteristics:

- *Finger pressure therapy* is an Oriental healing method wherein a practitioner applies pressure to specified points on the body to restore energetic balance to the body, mind, and spirit.

- Every being is animated by a vital life force or energy called **Ki** (in Japanese), which circulates in the body through a series of channels called **meridians.**

- Disturbance or disharmony of the flow of *Ki* causes disease.

- Pressure points used in shiatsu are the same one used by an acupuncturist to insert needles.

- Shiatsu is performed with the client lying on the floor on a comfortable futon or cushion.

Specialized shiatsu designations include the following:

- Barefoot shiatsu

- Magnetic shiatsu

- Five-element shiatsu

Acupuncture

- Only a specially licensed **acupuncturist** can perform acupuncture.

- Needles are inserted into the meridian energy system.

- Chinese doctors are having incredible results.

- I recommend finding a very good *acupuncturist* doctor to cross-market with in your spa/salon.

Moxibustion

- **Moxibustion,** which lies between shiatsu and acupuncture, is based on the application of heat, by igniting a herbal preparation.

- It stimulates the immune system.

- This is an art that can only be performed by someone well trained.

Jin Shin Do Bodymind Acupressure

Jin Shin Do Bodymind Acupressure combines gentle yet deep finger pressure on acupressure points with verbal body focusing and emotional processing techniques to help release physical and emotional tension and armoring.

Thai Massage

Thai massage has the following characteristics:

- It resembles techniques of shiatsu, with the practitioner applying pressure with the palms and fingers to release blockages and balance the energy along specified body pathways.

- The network of energy is more closely linked to the Hindu energetic system of ***nadis*** than to the Chinese system of meridians.

- Thai massage uses a series of passive stretching to energize and increase range of motion.

Tuina-Traditional Chinese System of Manual Therapy

- Pronounced *t-weigh na;* it is an ancient Chinese system of manual therapies to facilitate healing by regulating the circulation of blood and *Ki,* which controls body function and enhances resistance to disease.
- The Beijing Special Massage Hospital treats more than 100,000 patients a year.

Reflexology

- Reflexology is a technique of manipulating various reflex areas of the body, mainly the feet.
- We have *reflex zones* in the feet that are related to body parts, organs, and glands.
- It can relieve areas of congestion through using thumbs and fingers to apply a series of manipulative strokes, which relaxes the foot and breaks up areas of tension.
- It improves circulation and increases relaxation.

Aromatherapy Massage

- Aromatherapy massage can be incorporated into nearly any type of massage technique.
- Essential oils can be absorbed through the skin; combine essential oil in a carrier oil.
- Once oils are absorbed by the skin, they are transported through the body's blood and lymphatic system to organs, glands, nerves, and soft tissue.

Energetic Bodywork

- Energetic bodywork influences the subtle, invisible, electromagnetic flow of energy that surrounds and infuses the body—referred to as the *human energy field* or *aura* (subtle body). This life energy is known as:

  Chi—Chinese

  Ki—Japanese

Prana—Sanskrit

Orgone—Reichian theory

Bioplasm—Soviet research

- Energetic bodywork includes a variety of healing traditions, including Chinese medicine, Indian ayurveda, Tibetan Buddhism, and Western metaphysics.

- It is complemented by quantum physics, **psychoneuroimmunology** (specialized field of research that studies the relationship between the brain and the immune system and how they communicate with each other using various chemical messengers), vibrational medicine, and energetic medicine.

Therapeutic Touch

- Therapeutic touch uses the first healing modality of its kind to be taught within a fully accredited master's degree program.

- Dolores Krieger, PhD, RN, Professor Emerita of Nursing at New York University's prestigious Division of Nursing, and Dora Kunz, a noted metaphysician, developed therapeutic touch.

Four Stages to Therapeutic Touch

1. Centers—to be in a state of stillness.

2. Assessing—healer feels for imbalances in the energy field (hot or cold/tingling sensation); healers experience different feelings, colors, sounds, and sensations.

3. Unruffling—clearing the clients energy field and releasing blocked energy that has become congested; energy will flow freely.

4. Transferring energy—once the field has been cleared, the practitioner transfers energy to the client, energy from the universe/divine.

A growing number of massage therapist and bodyworkers incorporate therapeutic touch into their work.

Craniosacral Therapy

- **Craniosacral therapy** is a hands-on approach system that extends from the skull, face, and mouth (the cranium) down and within the spinal column to the sacrum and coccyx.

- At the center of this network is the cerebrospinal fluid (CSF), which circulates throughout the system within an envelope of

FUNDAMENTAL PRINCIPLES OF THERAPEUTIC TOUCH

Therapeutic touch is based on two fundamental principles:

1. Each human being is an open energy system in dynamic relationship with the environment.

   Energy enters this system, circulates through, and then leaves.

   According to the ancient teachings of India, everyone is endowed with a set of seven major Chakras, which are nonphysical energy centers.

   Each Chakra is positioned strategically at a vital area of the human energy field.

   Chakras take in and transform prana for use by the body.

   According to their theory, prana enters through the spleen Chakra, passes through a interconnection of channels, and leaves the body through the shoulders, arms, and then out the center of the palms.

   Our palms are secondary Chakras—important healing energy centers.

2. Each individual is bilaterally symmetric, with right and left sides of the body mirroring each other.

   Ill people have depleted and disorganized energy.

   Healthy people have excess energy that is better integrated (people with charismatic personalities, actors, and public speakers often make excellent healers).

   A practitioner can detect energy imbalances from one side of the body to the other, based on cues in the energy field.

   The role of the healer in therapeutic touch is to be a vehicle for the transfer of energy to the weak or ill person, thereby being supportive to the healing process.

   All living organisms have an innate tendency to wholeness and order.

meninges, bathing, nourishing, and protecting the brain, the spinal cord, and the nerve roots.

- It originated early in the nineteenth century from a branch of the medical practice of osteopathy.
- The practitioner uses the bones and soft tissue of the skull and pelvis as handles to release tension areas.

Somato emotional Release

- Somato emotional release is based on belief that our bodies hold the energy of past traumas, both physical and emotional, in the form of memories in the body's physical tissue.

- With Somato emotional release the therapist finds and discharges energy that is embedded in congested areas as *energy cysts*.

Reiki

- **Reiki** (pronounced *Ray-key*) is an energetic healing practice that uses hands-on touch and focused visualization.
- It is a Japanese word meaning *universal life force*.
- Reiki practitioners use reiki energy to balance and amplify an individual's energy to promote healing.

Holotropic Breathwork

- *Holotropic* means *moving to wholeness*.
- Holotropic breathwork combines rapid deep breathing, evocative music, and focused bodywork.
- It can be done in individual or group sessions.
- It is beneficial for individuals seeking greater psychological unfolding or an expanded spiritual dimension in their life.

Polarity Therapy

- Polarity therapy rebalances the bipolar charge in a client's body (restores energetic balance).
- It addresses imbalances in the vital energy that animates the body, mind, and spirit.
- Ayurvedic tradition views all of life emanating from one single source of energy known as *Braham*.
- The head represents a positive pole of the body, and the feet represent a negative pole.
- It balances the rhythmic flow of energy between poles of positive and negative charge in the body.

Stone therapy is one of the most popular treatments offered in spas throughout the world. Combining massage strokes and alternating heat and cold stones, clients can enjoy stone therapy in massage, bodywork, facials, manicures, and pedicures. Stones work by resonating a specific energy, which when placed on the body removes blockages, stress, and negative energies. Regular Swedish, trigger point, and acupressure are great modalities to incorporate stones. Chakra stone therapy incorporates semiprecious stones on all seven Chakras or just specific areas you choose to focus on. The energy and mineral content, when used with essential oils, becomes a powerful synergy of *healing energy.*

Stone therapy is an ancient healing art rooted in Mayan civilization, Chinese medicine, and Egyptian rituals. In North America aboriginal people used stones in their sweat lodges, a practice that still thrives today. In 1994, Mary Nelson, a Tucson, Arizona-based massage therapist, rediscovered the ancient craft and called it *La Stone Therapy.* Since then, it has become the most demanded treatment in the spa industry in North America and has become extremely popular in Europe.

There are many types of massage and bodywork, which when personally experienced allow you to assess the process and benefits—then you can decide if you want to incorporate specific treatments in your facility. You can create "signature treatments" to offer your clients through educating and training yourself and your staff. Other options you may want to adopt include treatments for couples, seniors, children, and pregnant women.

Massage and bodywork can eliminate congestion by helping the body rid itself of stress, ease pain, and promote balance. Experts such as Deepak Chopra, Andrew Weil, Bernie Siegel, and Larry Dossey are all physicians who endorse the benefits of massage and other touch modalities.

The Challenges of the Future

One of the greatest challenges in the spa/salon industry is to continually be innovative and take advantage of any amenities that modernization has to offer. Consumers want something unique in terms of products, services, and treatments; they are tired of the same old thing.

Barb Higgins, coanchor and producer of CFCN News in Calgary, Alberta, Canada, has definitely found a spa that is anything but routine. For the last 10 years, Barb has visited Mexico to stay at the Rio Caliente Hotsprings Spa and Health Resort <www.riocaliente.com>, known for its unique treatments. "It's a rustic place but has wonderful Mexican charm," says Barb about the resort, a 45-minute drive from Guadalajara. Located on the bank of a river heated from a nearby volcano, the Rio Caliente (hot river) features a mixture of traditional and modern treatments, from steam rooms and mineral-rich pools to massages and reflexology. The resort also offers mud treatments, hiking paths, yoga classes, water aerobics, and horseback riding in a unique, laid-back spiritual atmosphere.

"Comfort is key," says Barb. "I don't tell everyone who's looking for a spa about this place. While it offers the services, it is really more of a retreat.

It is very tuned into the spiritual aspect of life, and for that reason I do not recommend it to people who are not bent that way. It is rustic and simple and that's the beauty of it."

Another challenge: How is it possible to help others heal when the healers are not taking care of themselves?

Cecilia Leatherberry, a legendary figure in the Canadian Professional Beauty Industry, the creator of Hair Arts and Sciences, shares her wisdom, "I have come to know that the law of life is service and that I have been blessed in crossing the paths of all in my walk of life, who serve so diligently and willingly to keep competitions a living art in the field of hairstyling. As we move forward in this century, so must we be aware that humanity's vibrations must be lifted from the density we live in today. As aestheticians and body therapists, much can be done in silent healing in addition to your massage therapy." Cecilia believes that in the beauty industry, hairstyling and aestheticians are one. "As we ourselves heal our bodies, mind, and emotions, the words we speak—this *upliftment*—will transmit to your clients through your hands and vibrations."

Our life journey is a process of evolving our consciousness, doing our personal work one step at a time, transforming like a butterfly, and shifting internally how we see the world and experience ourselves. Fully participating in our lives and trusting in divine timing and divine order allow us to trust in our own process, from which healing originates.

Beauty treatments have become total wellness packages. Clients will take a day or weekend spa package instead of a vacation. The diversity of customizing signature services and treatments to meet client demands will be evolving constantly. Having meditation rooms, specialized rooms to allow for speakers (herbalists, homeopathic doctors, plastic surgeons, cosmetic dentists, yoga, Pilates, healers, etc.) will prove to be holistic for your clients. Walking the labyrinth has become a path to tranquility and is being used to calm the minds of individuals when they need to make important decisions.

"I know of no more encouraging fact than the unquestionable ability
of man to elevate his life by conscious endeavor."

Henry David Thoreau

Embrace the transformations taking place in our society and gain insightful clarity to allow you to offer spa/salon experiences that will revitalize humanity. The body is a unified energy field: an integrated whole, where body, mind, and spirit are One.

Concepts for Consideration

1. How would you explain the benefits of infrared therapy to a client?
2. What type of water treatment process would you consider using in a spa/salon?
3. How would your place of business be affected if a client picked up a bacterium while having a service or treatment performed?
4. How do you as a professional take care of yourself physically, emotionally, intellectually, and spiritually?
5. How do you plan to keep abreast of the changes in the spa/salon marketplace, the advancing technologies in equipment and products, and the new world views?

A P P E N D I C E S

APPENDIX

Company Policy Manual

A. The Company
- Name
- Address
- Owner
- Background history
- Location(s)

B. Vision/Mission or Philosophy Statement
- Based on your beliefs and values

C. Services and Products Provided
- What you do and why—philosophy may be integrated

D. Company Responsibilities and Commitments
- To provide an application form when people request employment
- To conduct an assessment of skills and attitudes during the interview process of applicants
- On hiring, employees will have a contract and personal tax form to sign and will be given a copy of our Company Policy Manual.
- On hiring, employees will receive a Job Description that will be reviewed together for your benefit and clarification. The employee will be given a job performance evaluation after 30 days of employment, and then again in 3 months from that date. Depending on the evaluation outcome, scheduling of evaluations are every 6 months, eventually moving to once a year.

- On hiring, employees will go through orientation and training using our Procedures Manual, which outlines company standards and procedures for services. The Procedures Manual is reviewed and updated annually; it is company property and will not be removed from the facility.

- On hiring, the employer will require a copy of the employee's license and certification (dependent on specialized area) to keep on file.

- On hiring, the employer provides education, training, and personal development opportunities for staff.

- On hiring, the employer will work with the employee individually to develop personal and business goals and create an action plan to help the employee monitor and achieve success.

- The employer will provide a process for any work-related concerns that cannot be resolved with internal management so the employee can contact the next level of management.

- The employer will fully disclose all health/safety product handling rules.

- The employer will provide a safe work environment.

- The employer will support Provincial/State Health and Safety Legislation.

- The employer will support the Labor Board and Employment Standards Act, the Human Rights Code providing a fair and equitable work environment.

E. Employee Responsibilities and Commitments

- The employee will comply with local, provincial, federal, or state regulations for registration and renewal of licensing and certification.

- The employee will adhere to local, provincial, federal, or state Health and Safety Legislation and will agree to and follow the safe work policies and procedures posted in the facility.

- The employee will behave in a professional manner displaying measurable attributes of the following:

    Commitment

    Punctuality

    Enthusiasm

    Courteousness

    Helpfulness

Knowledge

Competent skill level

Articulation

Responsibility

Accountability

Caring and compassion

- The employee will sign our company contract agreeing to abide by our policies and procedures.

- The employee will acknowledge, understand, and fulfill the job description.

- The employee will project a fashionable and inspiring image that reflects current styles.

- The employee will attend all educational, training, and professional development in-house programs and conventions.

- The employee will complete data service records for clients and keep them maintained.

- The employee will build a clientele.

- The employee will offer clients home-maintenance products and explain the benefits, which will result in retail sales.

- The employee will experience salon and spa services and products, so that he or she may share the benefits with others.

- The employee will refrain from internal gossip with co-workers.

- The employee will be sensitive to clients needs, honoring their privacy and modesty.

- The employee will adhere to the standards of hygiene defined by the company.

- The employee will honor the confidentiality of the business and the client.

- The employee will be responsible for creating team spirit with co-workers.

- The employee will adhere to spa/salon dress code and appearance expectation. Come prepared to work with hair and makeup done.

- The employee will attend staff meetings (weekly, monthly).

F. Operating System

Hours of operation

Payroll

- Process (bank deposit)
- Date
- Payroll cycle
- Salary structure

    Salary

    Commission on service

    Commission on sales

    Bonuses

    Salary review

    Share options

- Employment status

    Full-time

    Temporary

    Part-time

- Absentee policy

    Doctor's note

- Holidays
- Breaks

Benefit package

- Medical
- Dental
- Day care program
- Savings plan

Employee discount program

- Services and products
- Discount for family members

Gift certificate system

- Company policy
- Timeframe
- Gift certificate services/or dollar value
- Tracking system
- Procedures to follow

Product return system

- Company policy

I acknowledge, understand, and agree to comply with all the company policies.

_____   _____   _____
Date   Employee Signature   Supervisor Signature

Employee Contract

Employee Contract

Between _____ and _____
(Employer)   (Employee)

The undersigned Employee hereby promises the Employer:

A. To keep the Employer's business secrets, including but not limited to customer, supplier, logistical, financial, research, marketing, and development information, confidential and to not disclose the Employer's business secrets to any third party during and after the term of the Employee's employment.

B. Specific account non-competition clause that, on the termination of the Employee's employment with the Employer for any reason, the Employee will not solicit any customer of the Employer, whether or not still a customer of the Employer and whether or not knowledge of the customer is considered confidential information, or in any way aid and assist any other person to solicit any such customer from the date of termination of the Employee's employment.

If any part of these promises is void for any reason, the undersigned accepts that it may be severed without affecting the validity or enforceability of the balance of the promises.

DATE _____

Signed and delivered in the presence of:

_____
{Signature of Employer}

_____
{Signature of Employee}

_____   _____
{Signature of Witness}   {Witness—print name}

APPENDIX *Procedures Manual*

To provide consistent, professional services within the organization's timeline you need to describe in detail the procedures of the treatment and/or service timeframe and benefits. This is extremely important as a teaching tool for new staff as to the organization's expectations and as a reference guide for management.

The procedures manual is personalized to your specific services and treatments. I will give you an example of a format for a salon and for a spa service.

Color Foils
- Benefit/value
- Supplies
- Techniques
- Timeframe

Foot Therapy
- Benefit/value
- Supplies
- Traditional pedicure
- Spa pedicure
- Paraffin wax therapy

You will want to hire a consultant to write, design, and create a "customized" Procedures Manual for your "Signature Treatment and Services." To find a consultant, check with your distributors, search the Internet, or contact me at <www.kyron.ca>.

APPENDIX

Application for Employment

Application for Employment

Position applied for _____

Date available to start work _____

Certificate/License # (relevant to position applied for) _____

Name _____

| Last Name | First Name | Middle Name |

Address _____

| Street | City | Province/State | Postal/Zip |

S.I.N. _____

Resume included with Application for Employment ☐Yes ☐No

Are you applying for: _ Full-time _ Part-time

Hours available: Mon._____ Tues. _____ Wed. _____ Thurs. _____ Fri. _____ Sat. _____
Sun. _____

Why would you like to work with this organization?

_____

_____

_____

Work experience (List most recent)

Position _____   Dates of employment_____

Employer _____   Address _____

Responsibilities _____   Telephone _____

Wage _____   E-mail _____

Reasons for leaving _____   May we contact this employer? ☐Yes ☐No

Personal reference contacts (other than family) you have previously worked with that we can contact:

_____

Name   Occupation/Title   Telephone

_____

Name   Occupation/Title   Telephone

_____

Name   Occupation/Title   Telephone

Is there anything else you would like to tell us about yourself?

_____

_____

_____

_____

_____

I certify that all the information provided in this application is accurate and complete, and I understand that intentionally providing false information could result in refusal of employment or discharge. I authorize all persons named above to provide information regarding my employment qualifications and character.

_____

          Signature   Date

APPENDIX

Performance-Based Job Description

Aesthetician

Activities and Duties

- Building a clientele and performing services and treatments according to the Procedures Manual

- Greeting clients and performing analysis on the skin before the treatment. This helps you determine the type of facial or treatment and home-maintenance products for recommendation.

- Booking client for next appointment, depending on analysis or assessment, and scheduling a series of treatments

- Selling home-maintenance products, gift certificates, and promotions

- Assisting with laundry and general clean-up of facility

- Keeping treatment rooms clean, organized, and ready for use

- Learning about all the services and treatments available in the spa/salon, and their benefits, so you may market them

- Learning about all professional and retail products available in the spa/salon, and their benefits, so you may market them

- Attending staff meetings, in-house training, and conventions/trade shows to keep up with the trends

- Keeping in contact with clients, via the phone, sending cards, etc., to build and retain clients
- Keeping professional cabinet supplies stocked and organized
- Keeping changing rooms clean, with necessary robes, slippers, etc.
- Making sure clients have required water and lunches throughout the services
- Cleaning steam rooms, hydrotherapy tubs, and other equipment
- Attending promotion venues to market the business

Knowledge and Skills/Ability Requirements

- Ability to perform specific face, body, nail, and foot treatments and services
- Excellent interpersonal skills with clients, staff, and community
- Excellent communication skills: sensing, verbal and written
- Ability to learn and work effectively and quickly
- Ability to identify priorities, organize, and manage time effectively
- Ability to build relationships with clients and staff, built on trust, respect, skill competency, caring, and confidentiality
- Ability to upsell services and sell products
- Ability to read magazines and journals relevant to the industry
- Ability to represent the company in a positive manner
- Excellent presentation and image, immaculate personal grooming, specific "attire," comfortable shoes, and short fingernails

Performance Evaluation

- Performance will be evaluated after 30 days of employment, then again in 3 months
- Depending on the 3-month evaluation report outcome, scheduling of evaluations will be every 6 months, eventually moving to once a year
- Report to the Spa Director

Performance-Based Job Description

Stylist

Activities and Duties

- Building a clientele and performing services and treatments on clients according to the Procedures Manual

- Greeting clients, performing services, and updating information on client services

- Booking clients for next appointment

- Selling home-maintenance products, gift certificates, and promotions

- Assisting with laundry and general clean-up of facility

- Keeping styling station organized and clean

- Learning about all the services and treatments available in the spa/salon, and their benefits, so you may market them

- Learning about all professional and retail products available in the spa/salon, and their benefits, so you may market them

- Attending staff meetings, in-house training, and conventions/trade shows to keep up with the trends

- Keeping in contact with clients via the phone, sending cards, etc., to build and retail clients

- Keeping all displays stocked and clean
- Helping with inventory—professional and retail
- Attending promotion venues to market the business

Knowledge and Skills/Ability Requirements

- Ability to perform high-quality competency skills when working with clients
- Excellent interpersonal skills with clients, staff, and community
- Excellent communication skills: sensing, verbal and written
- Ability to learn and work effectively and quickly
- Ability to identify priorities, organize, and manage time effectively
- Ability to build relationships with clients and staff, built on trust, respect, skill competency, caring, and confidentiality
- Ability to upsell services and sell products
- Ability to read magazines and journals relevant to the industry
- Ability to represent the company in a positive manner
- Excellent presentation and image; fashionable, stylish dress, hair, and makeup

Performance Evaluation

- Performance will be evaluated after 30 days of employment, and then again in 3 months
- Depending on the 3-month evaluation report outcome, scheduling of evaluations will be every 6 months, eventually moving to once a year
- Report to Salon Manager/Director

Performance-Based Job Description

Massage Therapist

Activities and Duties

- Building a clientele and performing specific massage services and body treatments in accordance with the Procedures Manual

- Greeting clients, performing assessment on clients, filling in assessment forms, and completing insurance claim forms

- Booking clients for next appointment, depending on assessment, and scheduling a series of treatments

- Selling home-maintenance products, gift certificates, and promotions

- Assisting with laundry and general clean-up of facility

- Keeping treatment rooms clean, organized, and ready for use

- Learning about all the services and treatments available in the spa/salon, and their benefits, so you may market them

- Learning about all professional and retail products available in the spa/salon, and their benefits, so you may market them

- Attending staff meetings, in-house training, and conventions/trade shows to keep up with the new trends

- Keeping in contact with clients via phone, sending cards, etc. to build and retain clients

- Keeping professional cabinet supplies stocked and organized
- Keeping changing rooms clean and stocked with necessary robes, slippers, etc.
- Making sure clients have required water and lunches throughout services
- Cleaning steam rooms, hydrotherapy tubs, and other equipment
- Attending promotion venues to market the business

Knowledge and Skills/Ability Requirements

- Ability to perform specific massage treatments, body treatments, and spa services professionally
- Excellent interpersonal skills with clients, staff, and community
- Excellent communication skills: sensing, verbal and written, and ability to remain silent during treatment/service
- Ability to learn and work effectively and quickly
- Ability to identify priorities, organize, and manage time effectively
- Ability to build relationships with clients and staff, built on trust, respect, skill competency, caring, and confidentiality
- Ability to upsell services and sell products
- Ability to read magazines and journals relevant to the industry
- Ability to represent the company in a positive manner
- Excellent presentation and image, immaculate personal grooming, specific attire, comfortable shoes, and short fingernails

Performance Evaluation

- Performance will be evaluated after 30 days of employment, and then again in 3 months.
- Depending on the 3-month evaluation report outcome, scheduling of evaluations will be every 6 months, eventually moving to once a year.
- Report to Spa Director

Performance-Based Job Description

Activities and Duties

- Greeting clients, advising salon/spa staff their client has arrived; making the client comfortable, hanging their coats, helping them prepare for service
- Answering telephones, making appointments using an appointment book or management software package
- Filling in client data, updating data if necessary in database or filing system: service/treatment received, products used, and home-maintenance products purchased
- Opening and closing business, if applicable
- Booking client for next appointment
- Selling: retail products, gift certificates, promotions
- Balancing money at completion of shift
- Faxing menus to clients that request them
- Receiving inventory, checking inventory, pricing and/or bar coding
- Doing inventory on request
- Attending staff meetings and in-house training

- Keeping reception area clean and organized
- Keeping all displays stocked and cleaned
- Taking clients on facility tours

Knowledge and Skills/Ability Requirements

- Ability to operate multiline telephone
- Ability to operate a computer and the software program for booking appointments (or use an appointment book)
- Good communication skills, both verbal and written: speaks clearly, writes legibly
- Ability to learn quickly and multitask; if answering the telephone or booking an appointment, acknowledge walk-in client
- Ability to learn about all services and treatments that will enable you to explain the benefits, upsell, and book the appointments
- Ability to identify priorities, organize, and manage time effectively
- Ability to operate fax and photocopy equipment
- Ability to effectively handle all customers and staff, creating positive experiences
- Ability to represent the company in a positive manner
- Excellent presentation and image, fashionable, stylish dress, and excellent personal grooming

Performance Evaluation

- Performance will be evaluated after 30 days of employment, and then again in 3 months.
- Depending on the 3-month evaluation report outcomes, scheduling of evaluations will be every 6 months, eventually moving to once a year.
- Report to Spa/Salon Director

Performance-Based Job Description

Salon Manager/Director

Activities and Duties

Activities and duties involve the ability to supervise the day-to-day business salon operations, which include the following:

- Opening and closing facility
- Scheduling staff
- Monitoring customer service to ensure professional, high-quality experience
- Making daily deposits
- Maintaining a clean and safe environment
- Monitoring professional and retail inventory and daily supplies (office, cleaning, coffee, miscellaneous)
- Ordering products and supplies
- Analyzing reports on the types and numbers of services and treatments rendered to discuss with owner and create strategies to increase sales
- Recording payroll of employees, using the company system to give to the bookkeeper or payroll services
- Handling all customer-service complaints

- Understanding all services and treatments available in the spa/salon and their benefits so you can train and coach employees to team market services and treatments

- Understanding all professional and retail products available in the spa/salon and their benefits so you can train and coach employees and market the product

- Understanding all the systems that form the infrastructure of the organization

- Understanding and effectively implementing the marketing plan

- Monitoring all gift certificates using company system

- Being able to supervise, coach, and inspire employees to create a professional team

- Recruiting, interviewing, and hiring employees using the company procedures and systems

- Reviewing the job application, resume and contact references; on hiring review with the new employee the Policies Manual, Job Description, and Procedures Manual and set up relevant training and orientation

- Discerning behavior patterns of employees and effectively dealing with any challenges, such as absenteeism, negative attitude, etc.

- Monitoring performance and assessing the individual's performance using the performance evaluation system

- Guiding individual employees in setting up an action plan with measurable goals for building and retaining clientele, selling services and products, and personal development

- Monitoring and assessing the action plans of employees to see if they are achieving their goals and producing desired results

- Training and developing the employee so they actualize their potential and become an asset to the company

- Organizing and scheduling in-house training programs with suppliers on new styles, services, and product knowledge

- Organizing and scheduling staff meetings using a written agenda and doing follow-up so that effective results are created

Knowledge and Skills/Ability Requirements

- Leadership skills, with an in-depth understanding of human behavior and differences in individuals

- Basic business and management fundamentals

- Computer and software management skills relevant to the company's system
- Ability to operate fax and photocopy equipment
- Excellent interpersonal skills with clients, staff, community, and media
- Excellent communication skills: sensing, verbal and written; articulation and listening
- Organization skills, ability to plan, set priorities, delegate, and meet time and budget requirements
- Accountability and responsibility; extremely self-directed, displaying initiative, commitment, and loyalty to self and company
- Sensitive to staff issues, endorses staff development, and coaches and trains employees
- Maintains professionalism and a positive attitude, while adhering to company guidelines
- Ability to build relationships with staff, clients, community, and media based on trust, respect, skill competency, caring, and confidentiality
- Ability to keep up-to-date on all new services, products, and equipment through reading journals and magazines; attending conventions and trade shows; and accessing relevant information on the Internet
- Ability to learn and work effectively and quickly
- Ability to multitask, having an awareness and mindfulness of the big picture and the ability to handle stress
- Excellent presentation, physical health, and personal well-being and grooming
- Professional image with fashionable and stylish appearance in clothing, hairstyle, skin care, makeup, and nails
- Always represents the company in a positive, professional manner

Performance Evaluation

- Performance will be evaluated after 30 days of employment, and then again in 3 months.
- Depending on the 3-month evaluation report outcomes, scheduling of evaluations will be done every 6 months, eventually moving to once a year.
- Report to owner or Human Resource Department

Performance-Based Job Description

Spa Director

Activities and Duties

Activities and duties of the spa director involve the ability to supervise the day-to-day business of spa operations, which include the following:

- Opening and closing facility
- Scheduling staff
- Monitoring customer service to ensure professional, high-quality experiences
- Making daily deposits
- Maintaining a clean and safe environment with ambiance
- Monitoring professional and retail inventory and daily supplies: office, cleaning, coffee, lunches, candles, flowers, etc.
- Ordering products and supplies and working with sales representatives
- Analyzing reports on the types and numbers of services and treatments rendered; discussing with owner and creating strategies to increase sales
- Recording payroll of employees, using the company system to give to the bookkeeper or payroll services

- Handling all customer complaints

- Understanding how all spa equipment works in the spa so you can train employees

- Understanding all services and treatments available in the spa/salon and their benefits so you can train and coach employees and market services and treatments

- Understanding of all professional and retail products available in the spa/salon, and their benefits so you can train and coach employees and market the products

- Understanding all the systems that form the infrastructure of the organization

- Understanding and effectively implementing the marketing plan

- Creating, writing, and designing brochures and/or menus

- Monitoring all gift certificates and promotions using the company system

- Being able to supervise, coach, and inspire employees to create a professional team

- Recruiting, interviewing, and hiring employees using the company procedures and systems

- Reviewing the job application, resume, and contact references; on hiring reviewing with the new employee the Policies Manual, Job Description, and Procedures Manual and setting up relevant training and orientation

- Discerning behavior patterns of employees and effectively dealing with any challenges, such as absenteeism, negative attitudes, etc.

- Monitoring performance and assessing the individual's performance using the performance evaluation system

- Guiding individual employees in setting up an action plan with measurable goals for building and retaining clientele, selling services and products, and personal development

- Monitoring and assessing the action plans of employees to see if they are achieving their goals and producing desired results

- Training and developing the employee so they actualize their potential and become an asset to the company

- Organizing and scheduling in-house training programs with suppliers on new products, services, treatments, and equipment

- Organizing and scheduling staff meetings using a written agenda and doing follow up, so that effective results are created

Knowledge and Skills/Ability Requirements

- Knowledgeable and articulate in spa philosophies and wellness
- Have a Spa Director's certificate
- Exude a presence of spa savvy
- Knowledgeable and experienced in business fundamentals
- Strong leadership skills, with an in-depth understanding of human behavior and the differences in individuals
- Computer and software management skills relevant to the company's system
- Ability to operate fax, photocopy, and e-mail and visit Web sites on the Internet (the company's own or others)
- Excellent interpersonal skills with clients, staff, community service clubs, and media
- Excellent communication skills — sensing, verbal and written; articulation and listening
- Organization skills, ability to plan, set priorities, delegate, and meet time and budget requirements
- Accountability and responsibility; extremely self-directed, displaying initiative, commitment, and loyalty to self and company
- Sensitivity to staff issues: endorses staff development, and coaches and trains employees
- Maintains professionalism and a positive attitude, while adhering to company guidelines
- Ability to build relationships with staff, clients, community, and media built on trust, respect, skill-competency, caring, and confidentiality
- Ability to make presentations at public events, to corporations and service clubs, and to work closely with the media
- Ability to effectively write articles for the media
- Ability to keep up-to-date on all new services, treatments, products, and equipment for the spa by reading journals and magazines, attending conventions and trade shows, and accessing relevant information on the Internet
- Ability to learn and work effectively and quickly
- Ability to multitask, with an awareness and mindfulness of the big picture, and the ability to handle stress

- Excellent presentation, physical and emotional health, expressed as personal well-being
- Professional image with fashionable and stylish appearance in clothing, hairstyle, skin care, nails, and makeup
- Always represents the company in a positive, professional manner

Performance Evaluation

- Performance will be evaluated after 30 days of employment, and then again in 3 months.
- Depending on the 3-month evaluation report outcome, scheduling of evaluations will be done every 6 months, eventually moving to once a year.
- Report to owner or Human Resource Department

Employee Performance Evaluation

Employee Performance Evaluation

"What we measure gets improved." Peter Drucker

Employee Name _____ Title Position _____

Date Hired _____ Length of time in current position _____

Last Evaluation _____ Next scheduled evaluation _____

3. Employee's Responsibilities and Duties (attach job description)

Evaluation of Job Components	Excellent	Good	Fair	Poor
Attitude: Professional, positive attitude. Enthusiastic and mindful of meeting client needs and organization needs.				
Skill Competency: Understands techniques and requirements of position. Continually strives to improve and acquire new knowledge and skills.				
Customer Service: Professionalism in greeting, assisting, and being courteous to clients. Creates outstanding "client experiences."				
Client Retention: Expertise in building a clientele, follows through on booking appointments.				
Sales Skills: Ability to "upsell" services and share expertise with clients so they purchase home-maintenance products.				
Team Work: Ability to work well with co-workers and management; a willingness to help others.				
Accountability: Dependable and responsible, takes initiative to be self-directed, care for oneself, perform duties and stay on task.				
Organization Skills: Ability to manage time, set priorities and goals, creating results through action.				
*Leadership: Ability to inspire others "to do" and "to be" their very best. Excellent understanding of human behavior.				
*Supervisor: Sensitive yet strong on staff issues, includes staff development and training and coaching.				
*Business: In-depth understanding of business fundame... ...eets budget, and increases profitability of business.				
*Marketing: Implements marketing strategies, meets ...ing budget, and exemplifies creativity and innovation in product, service, treat... ...nd equipment research.				

*If applicable

Employee Performance Evaluation

Describe goals and accomplishment achieved within time frame being evaluated:

_____
_____
_____

Describe employee strengths:

_____
_____
_____

Describe performance and improvement needs:
Identify areas of improvement:

_____
_____
_____

Describe action plan and timeframe involved to improve areas:

_____
_____
_____

_____   _____   _____

Date   Supervisor Signature   Employee Signature

APPENDIX

Recruitment System

The job market is very competitive, with qualified candidates in high demand and consequently less available. Companies are looking to new and more creative ways of staffing. I believe companies also need to look within their organizations to identify why they have high staff turnover. Planning the recruitment process is important to ensure the right activities are undertaken to attract qualified staff.

What do you offer a new employee that would make them want to work with your organization?

- Benefits
- Job-sharing
- Higher wages
- Training programs
- Profit sharing
- Share options

Do not make false promises you cannot keep regarding training programs, bonuses, and incentives. Individuals in our industry are skeptical because of such broken promises.

The following is a range of options for identifying and attracting candidates to your company. Check the types of options you have used in the past and determine how effective they have been for you.

Options

_____ *Media Advertisement:* Local and national newspaper

_____ *Media Specific:* Trade journals and magazines

_____ *Job Postings:* Distributors, suppliers, schools; locally and nationally

_____ *On-Site:* Going to technical schools and academies to meet students

_____ *Employee Referrals:* an organization's own contacts and networks through employees

_____ *Special Events:* Career days at high schools, hospitality suites at conventions, job fairs

_____ *Employment Agencies:* Employment Insurance (E.I.) bulletin board and/or Web site posting; private employment agencies and directories have their own Web sites

_____ *Web Site:* Placing your advertisement on your own personal Web site

_____ *Associations:* Newsletters to aesthetic, health and wellness, hair, massage, and management associations

_____ *Walk-Ins:* Keep a file/record of candidates who make inquiries or drop off resumes

_____ *Industry Network:* An organization's own contacts and networks through industry associations, salespeople, and colleagues; candidates referred if moving

APPENDIX — *Interview System*

Employers are finding that the reliability of the interview process can be increased with the use of a structured interview format. A structured interview follows a predetermined plan of questioning. It means deciding ahead of time what subjects and topics are to be covered and why they are important.

The sequence of questioning need not be exactly the same because you want the interview to become informal conversation. I will give you a basic format and specific questions that you can use to meet specific position needs.

Here is a guideline for making the interview process more effective:

- Mention that the candidate was chosen to be interviewed based on skills and references.
- Carefully review the candidate's job application and resume.
- Ask open-ended questions.
- Move from general to more specific questioning.
- Let the applicant talk the majority of the time.
- Have a predetermined time allowed for the interview so other candidates with appointments do not wait and so you focus on the task.
- Keep an open mind, and be aware of how personal biases might affect the interview.

Choose from the series of questions that are relevant to the position.

- Why are you interested in our company?

- What experience do you have that you can apply to this position?

- What five words would you say describe you best?

- Why did you leave your last job? or Why do you want to leave your present job?

- What is your understanding of the nature of this job?

- What do you like the most about your profession?

- How do you react to instructions, feedback, or critiquing of your performance?

- What experience do you have in retail sales?

- What specific product knowledge do you have?

- What is your background in and understanding of spa philosophies?

- What experience do you have with using spa equipment? Specifically, Vichy shower, hydrotherapy, light therapy, and Swiss shower?

- What experience do you have with spa treatments and/or services? Specifically, microdermabrasion, mud treatments, stone massage, raindrop therapy, Watsu, and facials.

- How do you feel about working evenings and/or weekends?

- What strategies would you use to build a clientele?

- What are your long-range plans?

- What salary are you looking for?

- What previous business experience do you have?

- What do you think would be the most challenging aspect of this position?

- How would you describe marketing?

- What are some marketing strategies you would use to promote the business?

- What strategies would you use to build a team?

- Have you ever participated in an assessment processes?

- What do you feel is the value in assessment tools?

- What is your philosophy on health and well-being?

- What do you believe clients want most in our industry?

- How would you handle an employee who was constantly late?

- What experience do you have with performance evaluations?

- What knowledge and understanding do you have with creating signature spa treatments?

- What do you see yourself doing in 5 years?

- What is your knowledge of ayurvedic medicine, Chakras, and/or aromatherapy?

- What is your background and success in training?

- What is your philosophy on developing the human potential in individuals?

- What inspires or motivates you?

- What was the name of the last book you read?

- Do you enjoy being a spectator or playing a sport?

You can choose some of the questions that are applicable to the position you are interviewing for out of the list or come up with some of your own. The series of questions will make you think about what skills and qualities are relevant to the position. I suggest choosing no more than 10 questions. You will then need an assessment tool to identify and rate each candidate for his or her suitability for the position. I have given you a sample format that you can modify to your specific needs.

APPENDIX

Candidate Assessment Record

Candidate Assessment Record

Rank candidates: 1 to 5

5 – Excellent   4 – Very Good   3 – Good   2 – Fair   1 – Unsatisfactory

Interview Questions	A	B	C	D
	John	Kelsey	Elissa	Dylan
a. Why are you interested in our company?				
b. What is your understanding of the nature of this job?				
c. What five words would you say describe you best?				
d. What experience do you have that you can apply to this position?				
e. What is your background and understanding of spa philosophies?				

Rating Factors:	Comments
• Knowledge, skill, and ability required by specific position	A.
• Ability to understand and respond to questions	
• Attitude, professionalism	B.
• Customer service potential	C.
• Willingness to work with others	
	D.

Date _____   Interviewer _____

APPENDIX

Contract
Agreement

Contract Agreement

This contract for services is made in duplicate between:

(The "Hirer") _____

(include full name, address, phone and fax numbers, and e-mail)
AND

(The "Contractor") _____

(include full name, address, phone and fax numbers, and e-mail)

It is agreed that:

1. The Contractor will provide the Hirer with the following services as an independent contractor. Describe the "work" and "services" in detail.

2. The contractor will begin the work on _____
   day   month   year
   and substantially complete it by not later than _____
   day   month   year

3. The Contractor will pay a penalty of $_____ for late performance for each_____
   the work remains incomplete.   day/week/month

4. The total contract price (the "contract price") payable to the Contractor by the Hirer for doing the work, exclusive of any authorized extras, is $_____, which includes any necessary taxes (dependent on country, province, state).

5. Subject to any statutory holdbacks under any applicable construction or builders' lien legislation, the Hirer will pay the contract price as follows:
   Deposit: _____
   Draw: _____
   Draw: _____
   Final Payment: _____
   less 5% for holdback _____ which will be given in 30 days _____;
                              amount   date
   or 45 days _____; or _____.
                   date   specified timeframe

6. The Contractor is only liable to perform and the Hirer is only liable to pay for extra services that are authorized in writing, setting out the details of extra services and the price of extra services, which will be signed by both parties (authorized extras).

7. The Contractor warrants that he/she is fully insured and that the insurance is adequate to provide coverage for any injuries sustained by any person on the work site or for any property damaged during the course of the work done under this contract. (Check specific rulings within country, province, or state.)

8. "Timing" is the essence of this agreement.

9. The terms of this agreement may only be amended in writing by both parties.

10. This agreement is governed by the laws of
    the country _____
    the province _____
    the state _____

Signed on the _____ day of _____, 20____.

_____   _____
Hirer's Signature   Contractor's Signature
In the presence of:

_____   _____
for the Hirer   for the Contractor

Resources

Magazines

Beauty Beat & Spa

Subscriptions: info@canhair.com or (414) 923-1111

11 Spadina Road

Toronto, Ontario

Canada M5R2S9

Beauty Inc.

Official publication of the Beauty and Barber Supply Institute (BBSI)

Subscriptions: (800) 468-BBSI or <www.bsi.org>

Canadian Hairdresser

Subscriptions: (416) 923-1111

11 Spadina Road

Toronto, Ontario

Canada M5R2S9

Dayspa

Subscriptions: (800) 624-4196 or <www.dayspamag.com>

P.O. Box 10566

Riverton, NJ 08076-0566

Dermascope

Subscriptions: <www.dermascope.com>

2611 N. Beltline Rd., Suite 140

Sunnyvale, TX 75182

Les Nouvelles Esthetiques

Subscriptions: (800) 471-0229

306 Alcazar Ave.

Coral Gables, FL 33134

MEDIcal SPAS

Subscriptions: <www.spamanagement.com> or (514) 274-0004

P.O. Box 2699

Champlain, NY 12919

Salon Today

Subscriptions: <www.modernsalon.com> or (808) 808-2623

400 Knightsbridge Parkway

Palatine, IL 60069

Skin Inc.

Subscriptions: <www.skininc.com> or (630) 653-2155

3625 S. Schmale Road

Carol Stream, IL 60188-2787

Spa Canada

Subscriptions: <www.partnerspublishing.com> or (866) 450-9768

461 King Street, Suite 203

Fredricton, NB

Canada E3B1E5

Spa Management

Subscriptions: <www.spamanagement.com>

P.O. Box 2699

Champlain, NY 12919

Associations

Aesthetics' International Association

<www.beautyworks.com> or (877) 968-7539

P.O. Box 468

Kaufman, TX 75142

Allied Beauty Association (ABA)

<www.abacanada.com> or (905) 568-0158

450 Matheson Blvd. East

Unit 46

Missisauga, Ontario

Canada L4Z1RS

American Academy of Anti-Aging Medicine

<www.worldhealth.net> or (773) 528-4333

1510 W. Montana Street

Chicago, IL 60614

American Association of Cosmetology Schools (AACS)

<www.beautyschools.org> or (800) 831-1086

15825 N. 71 St., Suite 100

Scottsdale, AZ 85254-1521

Cosmetology Advancement Foundation (CAF)

<www.cosmetology.org> or (212) 750-2412

P.O. Box 811, FDR Station

New York, NY 10150-0811

Dayspa Association

<www.dayspaassociation.com> or (201) 865-2065

310 17th Street

Union City, NJ 07087

International SPA Association (ISPA)

<www.experienceispa.com> or (888) 651-4772

2365 Harrodsburg Road, Suite A325

Lexington, KY 40504-3335

**National Accrediting Commission
of Cosmetology Arts & Sciences (NACCAS)**

<www.naccas.org>

4401 Ford Avenue, Suite 1300

Alexandria, VA 22302

Society of Permanent Cosmetic Professionals

<www.spcp.org> or (847) 635-1300

69 North Broadway

Des Plaines, IL 60016

Spas Ontario Inc. The Association of Premier Spas

<www.spasontario.com> or (800) 990-7702

176 Napier Street

Barrie, Ontario

Canada L4M1W8

The Spa Association

<www.thespaassociation.com> or (970) 207-4293

P.O. Box 273283

Fort Collins, CO 80527

Web Sites

Virtual Salon for Hair, Skin, and Nail Care

<www.beautynet.com>

Trade show schedule continuing education calendar

<www.beautytech.com>

Milady/Salon Ovations' information on books, audiotapes and video-
tapes, computer software, etc.

<www.milady.com>

Spatech

<spatech@sympatico.ca>

Glossary of Terms

A

Absolute essence: the unique combination of a plant's life force that can function to reestablish mental and physical balance within an individual.

Acupuncturist: a specially licensed therapist, who inserts needles into the meridian energy system.

Alchemy: physical process to convert base metals such as lead to gold; an ancient path of transformation and spiritual purification, which expands the consciousness and develops insight and intuition.

Algae therapy: a collection of seaweed treatments used for therapeutic body treatments.

Alpha waves: brain waves present when normal individuals are awake in a resting state; waves with a frequency of 8 to 13 Hertz.

Aromacology: the study of aromas.

Aromatherapy: the application of the knowledge of aromas to heal by stimulating the nasal/olfactory senses, mental responses, and circulatory and respiratory functions.

Asklepeions: Greek center for healing and nurturing, named for Asklepios, who was a revered healer and philosopher of pre-Trojan wars.

Assessment tool: an instrument that identifies individual differences in people.

Atoms: particles moving at lightning speed around huge empty spaces that emerge from a field of pure energy or potentiality.

Aura: the external manifestation of the subtle or etheric body that is made up of the more spiritual aspects of oneself, experienced as thoughts, feelings, and emotions.

Ayurveda: a type of medicine practiced in India for more than 5,000 years that identifies a person's constitution and treats the person with diet, exercise, meditation, herbs, massage, sun, and breathing to bring harmony to the physical, mental, and spiritual health of the individual.

B

Baby Boomer: a member of the larger-than-expected generation born shortly after World War II.

Balance sheet: a financial document that gives you the financial position of the business, the assets, and where the money came from and what you did with the money.

Balneotherapy: a water therapy that uses fresh water.

Beta waves: brain waves present when the nervous system is active and when there is sensory input and mental activity; waves with a frequency of 14 to 30 Hertz.

Branding: a marketing process that identifies and positions your business in a very distinctive way in the marketplace.

Business plan: a document that summarizes the operational and financial objectives of a business and contains the detailed plans and budgets showing how the objectives are to be realized.

C

Cash flow: defines all cash received from all sources within a specified time period and what you have to pay out in that specified time period.

Chakra: is a Sanskrit word meaning wheel or disk and refers to seven basic energy centers with the body called the subtle or etheric body. Chakras are not to be thought of as synonymous with any portion of the physical body; they are superimposed on the physical body as an electromagnetic field. The seven Chakras are associated with the endocrine glands, a particular group of nerves called a plexus, and nerve ganglia, where there is a high degree of nervous activity.

Change masters: powerful and authentic individuals who have experienced life and use their intuition when making choices and decisions.

Chi: life force energy.

Chlorine: a nonmetallic element that is found alone as a strong-smelling, greenish–yellow irritating gas that is used as a bleach, oxidizing agent, and disinfectant.

Coach: to instruct, direct, or prompt.

Consciousness: awareness, cognizance, and knowingness.

Co-op advertising: when some manufactures share the cost of advertising with the business owner.

Craniosacral therapy: a hands-on approach system that extends from the skull, face, and mouth (the cranium) down and within the spinal column to the sacrum and coccyx.

Crystal therapy: an ancient healing art using crystals.

D

Delta waves: brain waves present during deep sleep; waves with a frequency of 1 to 5 Hertz.

Demographics: the statistical characteristics of a human population.

Dermis: the middle layer of skin.

Discernment: a process involving perception, intuition, decision making, and action; the ability to differentiate between making choices and decisions.

Divine energy: active life force.

E

Echo kids: children of a Baby Boomer.

Electromagnetic medicine: a theory that matter is energy operating at different frequencies and that the electromagnetic energy flowing through the body could determine the level of an individual's health.

Emotional intelligence: social intelligence that has the ability to understand people and act wisely in human relations.

Endermologie: massage therapy that reduces the appearance of cellulite while defining the figure.

Endocrinology: the study of the endocrine system and its glands, which are chemical factories that create complex compounds called hormones.

Endorphin: a neurochemical occurring naturally in the brain and having analgesic qualities.

Energy medicine: a recent medical theory that states that all matter is really another form of energy.

Enkephalin: an endorphin having opiate qualities that occurs in the brain, spinal cord, and elsewhere.

Epidermis: the outer layer of the skin.

Essence energy: the active force of a substance distilled or extracted from another substance.

Etheric: celestial or heavenly; the regions of space.

Exfoliation: removal of dead skin cells.

F

Feng shui: the art of placement that is based on an instinctive and learned understanding of relationships in space.

Financial statement: a financial document comprised of the balance sheet and income statement.

Fixed cost: expenses that remain the same every month.

Frequency: the number of cycles per second of an alternating current; the number of waves (as of sound or electromagnetic energy) that pass a fixed point each second.

Futurist: an individual who studies different aspects of society and human development to discern the developing trends.

H

Hammam: Arabic for spreader of warmth; a method of cleansing with steam without bathing.

Hertz: a unit of frequency equal to one second per cycle.

Hormones: chemical substances formed in one organ or part of the body and carried in the blood to another organ or part which it stimulates to functional activity or secretion.

Hydrotherapy: any treatments using water as a primary facilitator.

I

Income statement: a financial statement that shows revenue, expenses, and profit during a given accounting period, usually either quarterly or yearly.

K

Ki: a vital life force or energy that animates every being (in Japanese).

L

Labyrinth: a tool that is unicursal with 7 or 11 circuits with one well-defined path leading to the center and then back out; created to walk on or use with the fingers.

Lease: a contract transferring real estate for a term of years at will for a specified rent.

Light therapy: the application of light rays to the skin for the treatment of disorders.

M

Marketing plan: a document that outlines the specific actions you intend to carry out to interest potential customers in your product and/or service and persuade them to buy the product and/or service.

Meditation: a process of quieting the mind, gaining access to our inner wisdom and compassion, and resolving our inner conflicts in the process.

Meridians: series of channels by which *Ki* circulates throughout the body.

Microdermabrasion: a new method of refining lines and skin rejuvenation performed by a machine.

Moxibustion: type of treatment that is based on the application of heat, by igniting an herbal preparation.

N

Nadis: energy channels within the subtle bodies.

Nouveauté: newness, novelty, change, and innovation.

O

Organically certified: assures that the raw materials are grown on certified organic farms and that no petrochemical fertilizers or pesticides have been used on the farm or during the handling or processing.

Oscillation: fluctuating and moving back and forth between two points.

Oxygen therapy: type of therapy in which oxygen is delivered farther and deeper into the cells and tissues, after being dissolved into the circulatory system and body fluids; promotes cellular healing.

Ozone: a bluish gaseous reactive form of oxygen that is formed naturally in the atmosphere and is used for disinfecting, deodorizing, and bleaching; pure and refreshing air.

P

Perception: a mindset we use to view the world and how we view ourselves; it is shaped by our experiences, education, and beliefs.

Photorejuvenation: the application of light rays for a procedure of skin rejuvenation.

Phytotherapy: science that uses the unscented parts of botanicals, such as vitamins, minerals, amino acids, proteins, and enzymes.

Power: integration from within.

Prana: where the Divine Concept of Oneness sustains the life force within.

Profit: revenue that is left over after subtracting the variable costs and a percentage of the fixed costs.

Psychoneuroimmunology: a specialized field of research that studies the relationship between the brain and the immune system and how they communicate with each other using various chemical messengers.

R

Raindrop therapy: a specialized massage with essential oils.

Rasul: an ancient Middle Eastern ritual that takes place in an ornately tiled steam room, which allows for the self-application of medicinal muds and a rain shower rinse.

Reiki: an energetic healing practice that uses hands-on touch and focused visualization.

S

Salon: an elegant drawing room; a fashionable shop (beauty).

Scoliosis: a physical finding in which curvature of the spine is present.

Self-bronzing: a product that gives the skin a bronze color when applied.

Self-tanning: a product that darkens the skin when applied.

Serotonin: a neurotransmitter in the brain that creates a positive effect on an individual's mood.

Skin brushing: a powerful therapy that affects the entire body, considering the skin is a major organ.

Sound frequency: refers to pitch, the high or low of sounds, and is measured in Hertz.

Spa: health through or by water.

Spa philosophy: a basic theory and belief concerning what a spa is and what a spa does.

Steam therapy: type of treatment of cellulite that is superior to body wraps in raising temperature.

Stone therapy: water vapor used as a treatment.

Strategic alliances: a specific union of individuals who work together to promote and build relationships that benefit all involved.

Strigiles: specialized spoonlike scrapers used by Greek athletes after training sessions—before bathing.

Sweat therapy: a part of hydrotherapeutic tradition in European and American spas that is used to prepare for massages to increase suppleness of the muscles and create a deep sense of relaxation in the body and mind.

Swiss shower: a water therapy treatment combining the use of stationary water jets, which are aimed at pressure areas of the body; the water alternates between cold and warm to stimulate circulation and relieve tension.

Synergist: therapsit who uses a gentle touch, which is not invasive and does not inflict pain, to encourage a client to a more pleasurable way of being.

T

Thalassotherapy: a water therapy that uses sea water and other products from the sea.

Thermal therapy: a water therapy that uses hot spring water.

Theta waves: brain waves dominant in children of ages 2 to 5 years with a frequency of 4 to 7 Hertz.

Thyroxine: natural hormone produced by the thyroid gland.

Tradeskill: an experiential, hands-on, common-sense, sixth-sense approach to business.

Transformation: a change in structure, appearance, or character.

Trend: a prevailing tendency.

V

Variable cost: expenses that vary over the month.

Vibration frequency: the number of periodic oscillations, vibrations, or waves per unit of time.

Vibrational energy medicine: commonly thought of as acupuncture and homeopathy, therapeutic methods that apply frequency information directly to the body with electricity, sound, color, and lights.

Vichy: a water therapy treatment that incorporates a multi-jet rainbar that is suspended over a wet bed/table and used in special treatments to bring the body into balance.

W

Watsu: water shiatsu performed in a pool with a therapist and the client.

World view: a way of arranging the infinite energy of the universe or information into a system that makes sense.

Y

Yang: one of two opposite energies attracting and balancing each other.

Yin: one of two opposite energies attracting and balancing each other.

Bibliography and Recommended Reading

Angelo, J. (1991). *Spiritual Healing*. Rockport, MA: Element Books Inc.

Anodea, J. (2001). *Wheels of Life*. St. Paul, MN: Llewellyn Publications.

Beck, M. (1998). *The Theory and Practice of Therapeutic Massage*. Clifton Park, NY: Milady Publishing.

Beck, N. (1998). *The Next Century: Why Canada Wins*. Toronto: Harper-Collins Canada Ltd.

Bennett-Goleman, T. (2001). *Emotional Alchemy: How the Mind Can Heal the Heart*. New York: Harmony Books.

Brennan, B. A. (1998). *Hands of Light*. New York: Bantam Books.

Campbell, D. (2001). *The Mozart Effect*. New York: Harper Collins Publishers Inc.

Chopra, D. (1993). *Ageless Body, Timeless Mind*. New York: Harmony Books.

Claire, T. (1995). *Bodywork*. New York: William Morrow and Company Inc.

Clow, B. H. (2002). *Liquid Light of Sex*. Santa Fe, NM: Bear & Company Publishing.

Covey, S. R. (1990). *The 7 Habits of Highly Effective People*. Simon & Schuster.

Foot, D. K., & Stoffman, D. (2000). *Boom, Bust & Echo 2000:* Profiting from the Demographic Shift in the New Millennium. North York, Canada: Stoddart Publishing.

Gerber, M. E. (1995). *The E-Myth*. New York: Harper Collins.

Gerber, R. (2001). *Vibrational Medicine,* 3rd ed. Santa Fe, NM: Bear & Company Publishing.

Gladwell, M. (2002). *The Tipping Point: How Little Things Can Make a Difference*. New York: Back Bay Books.

Hawkens, P. (1988). *Growing on a Business*. New York: Simon & Schuster.

Keegan, L., & Keegan, G. T. (1998). *Healing Waters*. New York: Berkley Books.

Kiyosaki, R. T., & Lechter S. L. (2001). *Rich Dad's Rich Kid Smart Kid: Giving Your Children a Financial Headstart*. New York: Warner Business Book.

Maister, D. H. (1997). *True Professionalism*. New York: Simon & Schuster.

Maltz, M. (1996). *Psycho-Cybernetics*. New York: Pocket Books.

Myss, C. (1996). *Anatomy of the Spirit*. New York: Harmony Books.

Naisbitt, J., & Aburdene, P. (1990). *Megatrends 2000: Ten New Directions for the 1990's*. New York: William Morrow and Co.

Paulson, G. L. (1991). *Kundalini and the Chakras*. St. Paul, MN: Llewellyn Publications.

Pearsall, P. (1998). *The Heart's Code: Tapping the Wisdom and Power of Our Heart Energy: The New Findings About Cellular Memories and Their Role in the Mind/Body/Spirit Connection*. New York: Broadway Books.

Popcorn, F., & Marigold, L. (1998). *Clicking*. New York: Harper Collins Publishers Inc.

Schaef, A. W. (1992). *Beyond Therapy, Beyond Science*. New York: Harper Collins Publishers.

Schula, D., & Blanchard, K. (1995). *Everyone's a Coach*. Grand Rapids, MI: Zondervan Publishing House.

Wauters, A. (1996). *Ambika's Guide to Healing and Wholeness*. London: Judy Piatkus Publishers.

INDEX